Steck Vaughn

FOCUS
ON SCIENCE

ISBN 0-7398-9153-7 © 2004 Harcourt Achieve Inc.

Harcourt Achieve

Rigby • Steck-Vaughn

www.HarcourtAchieve.com
1.800.531.5015

Contents

About the Program

Introduction to *Focus on Science*

Focus on Science has been developed with both students and teachers in mind. The program presents important science concepts in language that is comfortable for on-level readers, as well as readers who read as much as one year below grade level. The content is engaging, and students are given frequent opportunities to satisfy their natural curiosity and sense of wonder through hands-on activities. The consistent lesson, exercise, and activity pages allow students to focus upon developing their science understanding.

Developed in accordance with the *National Science Education Standards* and the *Benchmarks of Scientific Literacy*, *Focus on Science* presents meaningful science content in lessons that fit easily into any instructional schedule.

About the Student Editions

The individual features in *Focus on Science* have been designed to promote student success. Students will find the style appealing and the content easy to use. Controlled vocabulary, carefully selected illustrations, and meaningful science activities work together to provide a positive learning experience for students.

Format

The student's text has three units—Life Science, Earth Science, and Physical Science. Each unit and chapter opens with an appealing photograph and brief text that encourages reflection and discussion. The opening page of each chapter also introduces the large science concepts students will encounter in their reading and activities. Six lessons follow each chapter opener. Lessons present science concepts in terms that students can understand and use illustrations and photographs to strengthen the learning process.

Hands-On Activities

Because children learn science by doing science, each chapter in *Focus on Science* provides students with a meaningful hands-on activity. These activities have been designed to maximize learning, while minimizing the demand for equipment. Important science concepts are the foundation for each activity. Activities combine carefully selected language and illustrations to guide students in independent discovery and learning. They also offer opportunities to practice problem-solving and process skills within a reasonable amount of time and with few materials.

Readability

In most classrooms, students vary widely in their reading skill development. *Focus on Science* recognizes skill diversity and presents science concepts precisely, but in an engaging style. Consequently, students will find the content manageable and interesting.

The reading level is carefully controlled at or below grade level. Important terms are defined in context, and supporting charts, diagrams, illustrations, and photographs enhance comprehension.

Text	Reading Level
Level A	Grade 1
Level B	Grade 2
Level C	Grades 2–3
Level D	Grade 3
Level E	Grade 4
Level F	Grade 5

Vocabulary

Important science terms are highlighted in boldfaced type and defined in the context of the lesson in which they first appear. The words are also arranged alphabetically in the glossary.

Illustrations

For students who rely upon visual clues for better understanding of what they read, *Focus on Science* uses illustrations, photographs, diagrams, and charts to reinforce important terms and concepts.

Special Features

Several special features have been designed to foster student interest in science. To emphasize that inquiry is the driving force in science, lesson titles are presented as questions. The questions encourage students to recall prior learning, seek more information, and ask more questions.

To reveal how science leads us from one question to another, the final section of each exercise page poses a critical-thinking question whose answer cannot be found directly in the text at hand.

At levels C through F, to show students how clues can lead to understanding, each unit begins with an intriguing task. Simple clues follow the question, "What is it?" Students may answer that question independently, or, as scientists often do, with the cooperation of their peers.

Finally, to demonstrate that science is done by many people in many settings, a Career Page appears at the conclusion of each unit. Text and photographs introduce some of the interesting science careers students may choose to pursue.

Assessment and Evaluation

Students engaged in active learning need frequent opportunities to assess their progress. Each lesson in *Focus on Science* is followed by an exercise with several sections. The first sections evaluate students' understanding of terms and concepts within the lesson. Questions appear in the order in which their answers are presented in the text. The final section of the exercise offers students practice in critical thinking. Answers to objective and critical-thinking questions are provided in the Teacher's Guide.

Focus on Science recognizes that many students benefit from experience in taking standardized tests. Consequently, comprehensive chapter and unit tests are designed to assess student learning through multiple-choice questions.

About the Teacher's Guide

The separate Teacher's Guide includes
- instructional strategies for presenting chapters and units,
- suggestions for engaging students in chapter and unit studies,
- further strategies for presenting features such as hands-on activities and career pages,
- suggestions for concluding chapter and unit studies and establishing connections to other curricular areas, and
- convenient blackline masters that extend student learning. Supporting blackline masters are identified. Simple answer keys for exercises and tests are included.

Blackline Masters

Skills Program

A successful science student acquires valuable problem-solving and process skills. *Focus on Science* offers students opportunities to develop these skills through guided questioning and participation in carefully designed, enjoyable activities. A blackline master dedicated to problem-solving and process skill development accompanies each chapter.

Chapter Reviews

Students benefit from frequent opportunities to organize their learning and review concepts. Chapter reviews present science concepts in a format unlike other activities, giving students an opportunity to review their understanding in new ways. Each chapter review is presented on a blackline master for convenience and versatility.

Unit Projects

Special unit projects, presented on blackline masters, provide creative learning extensions. They are also designed to promote independent learning. Students will be able to work successfully with little guidance from a teacher. Older children may also be encouraged to assess their performance using the easy-to-implement rubrics included in the Teacher's Guide.

Letters to Families

Because family involvement contributes positively to every student's success, a letter introducing each chapter is offered on a blackline master. These letters, written in both English and Spanish, keep family members informed and offer specific suggestions for activities that support instructional goals.

Meet your state standards with free blackline masters and links to other materials at **www.HarcourtAchieve.com/AchievementZone**. Click **Steck-Vaughn Standards**.

National Science Education Standards and Benchmarks for Scientific Literacy

National Science Education Standards recognize the cognitive development of students. The Standards in this chart are preceded by the grade levels where they have been determined as most appropriate.

Most of the Benchmarks for Scientific Literacy fit naturally in the framework of Science Education Standards. In this chart, specific Benchmarks receive special recognition as related to, but independent from the Standards. These Benchmarks are marked with an asterisk*.

National Science Education Standards and Benchmarks for Scientific Literacy	Level A	Level B	Level C	Level D	Level E	Level F
Unifying concepts and processes in science						
K–8 Systems, order, and organization	4	4	2	1,3,4	1–3	1,2,6
K–8 Evidence, models, and explanation			2	1–7	1–8	2,5,6
K–8 Change, constancy, and measurement				3,4,5	2	6
K–8 Evolution and equilibrium		4		3	2	
K–8 Form and function	2	1,2		1,3,4	2,3	
Science as Inquiry						
K–8 Abilities necessary to do scientific inquiry	1–6	4,5,6	1,3,5,6	1,2,4	1,2,6,7	1,2,4–8
K–8 Understandings about scientific inquiry	5,6	4,5,6	5,6	3,5,6,7	3,4,5,8	1–7
Physical Science						
K–4 Properties of objects and materials	6		6	7		
K–4 Position and motion of objects		6		7		8
K–4 Light, heat, electricity, and magnetism	6	6	6	7		7
5–8 Changes in properties of matter	6					7
5–8 Motions and forces					8	
5–8 Transfer of energy		6	7		7	
Life Science						
K–4 Characteristics of organisms	1,2	1,2	1–4	1,2		
K–4 Life cycles of organisms	1	1,2	1,2,4	2		
K–4 Organisms and environments	1,2,4,5	1,2,4,5	1,2,4,5	3		4
5–8 Structure and function in living systems			1	4	1,3	1,2
5–8 Reproduction and heredity					1	1,2,3
5–8 Regulation and behavior					2	
5–8 Populations and ecosystems				4	4	4
5–8 Diversity and adaptations of organisms				4	2	
*Basic function				2,3	3	2,3
*Human development				2,3		3
*Learning				2		
*Human identity				2		

National Science Education Standards and Benchmarks for Scientific Literacy *(continued)*

National Science Education Standards and Benchmarks for Scientific Literacy	Level A	Level B	Level C	Level D	Level E	Level F
Earth and Space Science						
K–4 Properties of Earth materials		4,5	5	5	5	
K–4 Objects in the sky	4,5	5		6		6
K–4 Changes in Earth and sky	4,5	4,5	6	5,6		5,6
5–8 Structure of Earth system					4,5	5
5–8 Earth's history						5
5–8 Earth in the solar system				6		6
Science and Technology						
K–4 Abilities to distinguish between natural and human-made objects			7	6,7	5,7,8	
K–8 Abilities of technological design				7	8	
K–8 Understandings about science and technology			6	6,7	5,7,8	
Science in Personal and Social Perspectives						
K–8 Personal health	3	3	3			
*Human Organism	3	3	2	3	3	3
*Physical health	3	3	3	3	3	3
K–4 Characteristics and changes in populations						
*Group behavior				4,5		
K–4 Science and technology in local challenges			4,5,7			4,8
5–8 Populations, resources, and environments			6,7			
*Agriculture					1,5	
5–8 Natural hazards					5	
5–8 Science and technology in society					5	8
*Global interdependence				4,5		
History and Nature of Science						
K–8 Science as a human endeavor				1–7	1–8	8
*Science as a human endeavor				1–7	1–8	8

Content Themes

	Life Science	Earth Science	Physical Science
Level A	Plants are living things Animals are living things About your body	What Earth is like Looking at the sky	Everything is made of matter
Level B	Plants react to their surroundings Animals react to their surroundings How to stay well	Earth has changed over time The sun	Energy has many forms
Level C	Plants grow and change Animals grow and change Keeping bones and muscles healthy	Plants, animals, and people depend on one another Rocks, minerals, and soil Weather and the water cycle	People get energy and materials from natural and recycled resources
Level D	Plants can make their own food There are many kinds of animals We learn about the world through our senses	Communities of living things in an ecosystem Landforms and oceans The solar system	Light, sound, magnetism, and electricity
Level E	Plants have changed over time Animals have changed over time The body has many systems	Earth has many biomes Earth's resources Weather and weather prediction	Energy can change from one form to another There are six simple machines
Level F	Plants reproduce in different ways Animal cells can perform a variety of functions Your body has control systems	Plants and animals are interdependent The changing Earth The universe and deep space	Physical and chemical properties of matter Electricity and magnetism can produce electrical energy

Lesson Scope and Sequence

Unit 1—Life Science   Chapter 1 How Plants Live and Grow

Lesson 1	Lesson 2	Lesson 3	Lesson 4	Lesson 5	Lesson 6
Most plants have three parts.	Living things are made of cells.	Plants use photosynthesis to make food.	Food and water move through plants.	Plants react to their environment.	Many plants reproduce through seeds.

Chapter 2 How Animals Live and Grow

Lesson 1	Lesson 2	Lesson 3	Lesson 4	Lesson 5	Lesson 6
There are many kinds of animals.	There are several ways to group animals.	Animals need food, water, and oxygen to live.	Animals have life cycles.	Humans are mammals.	Characteristics may be inherited or learned.

Chapter 3 Your Senses

Lesson 1	Lesson 2	Lesson 3	Lesson 4	Lesson 5	Lesson 6
You learn about the world through your senses.	Seeing is one of your senses.	Hearing is one of your senses.	Taste and smell are senses.	Touch is a sense.	You can keep your senses healthy.

Unit 2—Earth Science   Chapter 4 The Living Earth

Lesson 1	Lesson 2	Lesson 3	Lesson 4	Lesson 5	Lesson 6
An ecosystem is a community of plants and animals.	Plants are producers; animals are consumers.	Plants and animals compete to stay alive.	Ecosystems change.	People can change ecosystems.	People can protect ecosystems.

Chapter 5 Earth's Surface

Lesson 1	Lesson 2	Lesson 3	Lesson 4	Lesson 5	Lesson 6
A landform is a shape on Earth's surface.	Landforms can change slowly.	Landforms can change quickly.	Rocks form in different ways.	Water covers three-fourths of Earth.	People affect the ocean.

Chapter 6 Our Solar System

Lesson 1	Lesson 2	Lesson 3	Lesson 4	Lesson 5	Lesson 6
Astronomers use different tools to look into the sky.	The solar system is the sun and everything that circles it.	The moon orbits Earth.	The inner planets are four planets that orbit closest to the sun.	The outer planets are five planets that orbit farthest from the sun.	Meteoroids, asteroids, and comets are objects in our solar system.

Unit 3—Physical Science   Chapter 7 Energy

Lesson 1	Lesson 2	Lesson 3	Lesson 4	Lesson 5	Lesson 6
Light gives every object its color.	Light travels in a straight line until it strikes an object.	Sound is produced when an object vibrates.	Magnets pull or push other magnets or pieces of metal.	Electricity is used to make light, heat, and sound.	Electricity travels in electrical circuits.

Master Materials List for Hands-On Activities

Please pay particular attention when students are using sharp objects and/or handling hazardous materials in the Hands-On Activities. Advise them to use such materials cautiously.

Activity	Materials and Quantities	Special Notes
Chapter 1 **Watch a Plant in Action** (p. 20)	cups—several for the class to share spoon—several per class water—to fill cups red or blue food coloring—3 bottles celery with leaves—1 stalk for each student	Water is also required in Chapter 5. Paper and pencil are also required.
Chapter 2 **Watch Animals in Action** (p. 36)	fish in a tank or bowl—1 fish for the class fish food—1 container for the class lined paper—1 piece for each student pencil—1 for each student ruler—1 for each student	Paper and pencil are also required in Chapter 3. A ruler is also required in Chapter 6.
Chapter 3 **Use Your Sense of Touch** (p. 52)	paper bag containing mystery objects— several bags for the class to share lined paper—1 for each student pencil—1 for each student	Mystery objects could include marbles, blocks, toys, pencils, erasers, and salt shakers.
Chapter 4 **Watch an Ecosystem** **in Action** (p. 70)	meterstick—4 for the class to share wooden sticks—4 for each student string—2 balls for the class to share hand lens—1 for each student lined paper—1 for each student pencil—1 for each student scissors—2 for the class to share	You may wish to cut the string in 5-meter lengths before the activity. The string must be long enough to loop around the sticks and tie.
Chapter 5 **Observe Erosion** (p. 86)	large pan—1 for each group of 4 students sand—enough to fill pans water—enough to moisten sand drinking straw—1 for each student	

Chapter 6
Make a Solar System Model
(p. 102)
	blue and green markers—2 pairs for each
	    group of 4 students
	table tennis balls—2 for each group of
	    4 students
	balloons—4 for each group of 4 students
	red and blue clay—enough clay for each
	    group of 4 students to make
	    3 marble–sized balls
	ruler—1 for each group of 4 students
	tape—1 roll
	construction paper—1 sheet for each
	    group of 4 students
		Balloons should be orange, yellow, light blue, and dark blue.

Chapter 7 **Make a Telephone** (p. 120)	dental floss or fishing line—15 feet for each student pair paper clips—3 for each student pair paper cups—2 for each student pair	Six-ounce cups work well.

Unit Summary All living things are made of cells. Plants and animals need food to live and grow. Plants make their own food using photosynthesis. Animals must eat to get food. People use their senses to learn about the world around them.

Before Reading the Unit Have students look at the picture on page 5. Ask students what the living things in the picture need to live and grow. Then, ask students what each of them needs to live and grow. Guide the discussion to the basic needs of food, water, and a favorable environment. Have students read the text on page 5 and suggest they keep in mind the basic needs of plants and animals as they read the unit.

Unit Performance Project

Setup and Presentation Page 47 in this Teacher's Guide is a reproducible project that focuses on life cycles. Before you present the project, you may want to engage students in a short discussion of storyboards and other methods of illustrating text. Present the project to students after they have studied plant life cycles (Chapter 1, Lesson 6) or animal life cycles (Chapter 2, Lesson 4).

Evaluation A satisfactory project should show several steps in a life cycle of either a plant or an animal.

A good project should show several plant or animal life cycle steps. Steps would be in sequence and accurately identified.

An outstanding project should show all stages in the life cycle, each represented by a picture or drawing. Each stage should be correctly identified and should be accompanied by a brief description or explanation. There is a rubric on page 50 in this Teacher's Guide that will assist students in evaluating their own work on the unit performance project.

Careers Feature

Page 54 of the student text offers students a glimpse into these careers: horticulturist, entomologist, and pharmacist. Point out to students that people in these careers generally go on after high school to complete four years of college. Some may even acquire advanced degrees. Students interested in these fields should be encouraged to take science courses, particularly botany, biology, and chemistry. Ask students to think of other qualifications a horticulturist, an entomologist, or a pharmacist would need. (patience, excellent data collection skills) Suggest students choose one of the fields to research. Have them consult recent periodicals or the Internet to learn about developments in the field that have occurred within the last twelve months. Have students write a brief summary of information they find.

Unit Test The Blackline Master for Unit 1 Test is on page 41 of the Teacher's Guide. The test is in the standardized test format to provide students with practice in taking standardized tests. The unit test content focuses on life processes, life cycles, and cells as the basic units of life. The test also covers some basic information about human senses.

Answers: 1. C 2. D 3. B 4. C 5. A 6. A 7. B 8. B 9. D 10. A

After Reading the Unit Engage students in a discussion about how they can use the information they learned in this unit in their everyday lives. How does knowing about life cycles help them understand plants? How does it help them understand animals? Ask students to explain how the information in this chapter might make them change their behavior in some way.

Chapter Summary Most plants have roots, stems, and leaves, and are made of cells. Plants use energy from the sun to make their own food during photosynthesis. Plants move food, water, and nutrients through special structures called xylem and phloem. Plants respond to changes in their environment. Different plants reproduce in different ways. Flowering plants use flowers, and conifers use cones.

Chapter Objectives Students will learn to
- identify the basic parts of a plant.
- recognize that all living things are made of cells.
- explain how plants use photosynthesis to make food.
- relate how xylem and phloem move materials through plants.
- understand how plants react to their environment.
- understand how plants reproduce.

Vocabulary

roots, p. 8	stomata, p. 12
stems, p. 8	oxygen, p. 12
leaves, p. 8	xylem, p. 14
cells, p. 10	phloem, p. 14
microscope, p. 10	nutrients, p. 14
tissues, p. 10	life cycle, p. 18
organization, p. 10	reproduce, p. 18
process, p. 12	flowering plants, p. 18
photosynthesis, p. 12	pollen, p. 18
carbon dioxide, p. 12	eggs, p. 18
chlorophyll, p. 12	conifers, p. 18

Vocabulary Activity Help students create a classroom bulletin board diagram of a plant as they work through Lesson 1. Have them leave room for details such as cell diagrams and flowers. Have students make index card labels of vocabulary words to affix to the diagram.

Before Reading the Chapter Ask students to volunteer answers to the "What Is It?" riddle in the Chapter Opener. Then, if you have plants in the classroom, ask students to describe them. Encourage students to look for similarities and differences. Ask students what the plants need to live. Write student responses on the chalkboard. Allow students to revise their answers as they read the chapter.

Lesson 1 What Are the Parts of Plants?
Discuss how tall trees and small plants have the same basic parts. Ask students to tell how the stem of an oak tree and the stem of a dandelion are different. (The stem of a tall tree is hard and covered with bark. The stem of a small plant is thin and bends easily.) Then, ask students how the stems are alike. (Both help hold the plants up.)
Answers page 9: A. 1. leaves 2. soil 3. stems 4. food B. labels in order from the top: leaves, stem, roots C. The roots hold the tree in the soil and keep it from falling over.

Lesson 2 What Are Cells?
If a microscope is available, have students look at onion skin cells. Prepare a slide by placing a sliver of onion skin in a drop of water on the slide. Then, place a coverslip over the onion skin. Students should be able to see onion skin cells through the microscope. Ask students how the onion cells are part of the onion plant's organization. (Groups of onion cells make up onion tissue.)
Answers page 11: A. 1. cells 2. microscope 3. tissues B. 1. True 2. False 3. True C. cells, tissues, leaves, plants D. Cells are like bricks in that they are parts of larger things. A cell is a small part of a living thing. A brick is not living.

Lesson 3 How Do Plants Get Energy?
Explain that carbon dioxide, like oxygen, is part of the air around us. Plants use carbon dioxide, light, and water during photosynthesis. Plants make food and release oxygen. Ask students how photosynthesis might be expressed as an equation. Draw the first half of the equation on the chalkboard, and have students complete the equation. (light + water + carbon dioxide = sugar + oxygen)

Answers page 13: A. 1. food 2. chlorophyll 3. photosynthesis 4. carbon dioxide 5. oxygen 6. plants B. 1. Roots take in water from the ground. 2. Stomata let carbon dioxide enter the plant. 3. Chlorophyll traps light from the sun. 4. Oxygen moves from the plant into the air. C. Light is important to plants because plants use light to make their own food.

Lesson 4 How Do Materials Move Through Plants?

Ask students why they eat food. Help students see that they eat food to get nutrients. Explain that plants, too, need nutrients. They get them from the soil. Prompt a discussion about how plant parts not near the soil get nutrients. Encourage responses that suggest plants have a way to transport nutrients.

Answers page 15: A. 1. xylem 2. phloem 3. both 4. phloem B. Drawings should show a plant with stems, roots, and leaves. Students should use arrows to show that food moves through phloem in two directions, downward to roots and upward to leaves. Water and nutrients move upward from roots to stems and leaves through xylem. C. Answers will vary. Students might say that sweet liquid contains sugar. Because students know that food in plants is a kind of sugar, and food travels through phloem, they should conclude that the sweet liquid comes from the phloem.

Lesson 5 How Do Plants Grow and Change?

Point out that we respond to our environment. For example, we wear boots when it rains and a sweater when it is cold. Indicate that plants also respond to their environment. Engage students in a discussion about some of the changes they have observed in plants (flowering, leaves dropping, new growth in spring).

Answers page 17: A. 1. False 2. False 3. True 4. True B. 1. light 2. the center of Earth 3. water C. 1. √ 3. √ D. Food is made in leaves. Plants use food to grow.

Lesson 6 How Do Plants Reproduce?

Bring in a plant with seeds or a flower with reproductive parts that are easily identifiable. A large sunflower or a dandelion with seeds at the ends of the tufts offer simple examples for students to observe. Engage students in a discussion of what they observe.

Answers page 19: A. 1. a life cycle 2. adults 3. pollen 4. cones 5. female B. 1. Female parts of flowering plants make eggs. 2. Conifers make male and female cones. 3. Male parts of flowering plants make pollen. C. Answers will vary. Students might answer that squirrels might carry seeds away from trees and bury them. Seeds may also stick to the squirrels' fur. Seeds could possibly grow in the places where squirrels bury them or they drop from the squirrels' fur.

Hands-On Activity *page 20* Students will

engage in the process skill of observing as they watch how water moves through a plant. Cut celery stalks about 5 inches long. Red or blue food coloring works best. Have students wait about 4 hours or overnight to check the results. Students should see that the inside of the celery stem is red or blue. Students may want to draw a diagram to illustrate their written description.

Answers: 1. The colored water went into the leaves. I can tell because the leaves turned red (or blue). 2. Water moves through a plant's xylem.

Blackline Masters for Chapter 1:

Problem Solving Skills, page 27; Chapter Review, page 34; Letter to Family (English), page 51; Letter to Family (Spanish), page 52

"What Is It?" *Answer:* cell

Chapter Test *page 21*

Answers: 1. C 2. B 3. D 4. D 5. A 6. B 7. A 8. A 9. C 10. A

After Reading the Chapter

Art Have students make drawings or paintings of plants in the classroom. If possible, find a potted flowering plant, such as a primrose. Students can also paint or draw plants outside the classroom, such as trees or bushes.
Writing Tell students to imagine that they are inside a miniaturized car or truck that is too small to see without a microscope. Have them write a story describing a journey through a plant in this car or truck. Suggest that they use information in the chapter when writing their story.

Chapter Summary Animals are made of cells. Animals eat other animals or plants to survive. Animals can be grouped in many ways, such as whether they live on land or in water. Animals must have food, water, and oxygen to live. They digest food to get energy. All animals have a four-stage life cycle and begin as eggs. The human life cycle is egg, baby, child, adult. Adult animals can reproduce. Animals inherit some characteristics from their parents and learn other characteristics during their lifetimes.

Chapter Objectives Students will learn to
- describe and compare animals.
- identify how animals are grouped.
- understand how animals use oxygen, water, and food.
- identify the stages in the life cycles of some animals.
- explain the stages of the human life cycle.
- distinguish between inherited and learned characteristics.

Vocabulary

organs, p. 24	exoskeleton, p. 26
skin, p. 24	digest, p. 28
skeleton, p. 24	stomach, p. 28
cold-blooded, p. 26	intestines, p. 28
warm-blooded, p. 26	mammals, p. 32
vertebrates, p. 26	characteristics, p. 34
invertebrates, p. 26	inherit, p. 34

Vocabulary Activity Have students make word webs using groups of related terms. Some webs could include *organs, skin, skeleton, stomach; invertebrates, exoskeleton, cold-blooded; digest, stomach, organs, intestines.* After students have completed their webs, have them form small groups and discuss the meanings of the words and how they relate to one another.

Before Reading the Chapter Ask students to volunteer answers to the "What Is It?" riddle in the Chapter Opener. Then, have students discuss how animals include many varieties of living things, such as humans, mosquitoes, seagulls, bats, and trout. Ask students to name different kinds of animals. Write their responses on the chalkboard. Then, ask students to revise their answers as they read the chapter.

Lesson 1 What Are Animals?
Ask students to describe how animals are both similar to and different from plants. Record student responses. After students read the lesson, encourage them to revise their descriptions.

Answers page 25: A. 1. False 2. False 3. True 4. False 5. True 6. True B. 1. cells 2. organs 3. the skin 4. skeletons C. Students should list four of the following similarities between a whale and a mite. Both are animals. Both are made of cells. Both can reproduce. Both must eat plants or animals to get food. Both can move from place to place. Both have organs.

Lesson 2 How Are Animals Grouped?
Open the lesson by asking students to suggest ways that animals might be grouped. Have students bring photographs of different animals to class. Help them make a classroom bulletin board and place their photos in groups. Ask students to make a label caption that describes each group. After they've read the lesson, encourage students to change their labels or captions using the groups named in the text.

Answers page 27: A. 1. land animal 2. land animal 3. water animal 4. water animal B. 1. warm-blooded 2. cold-blooded 3. warm-blooded 4. cold-blooded C. 1. vertebrate 2. invertebrate 3. vertebrate 4. vertebrate D. 1. land animal 2. warm-blooded 3. vertebrate

Lesson 3 How Do Animals Use Oxygen, Water, and Food?
Introduce the lesson by pointing out that while students may notice if they are getting enough food, they may not know if they are eating the right kinds of foods. Then, have students read the lesson and study the diagram.

Answers page 29: A. 1. food 2. oxygen 3. two-thirds 4. digest 5. food B. 1. intestines 2. mouth 3. stomach C. 1. They get water from their food. 2. Students might mention that they would look for oxygen, water, and some kind of food, because all animals need them to survive.

Lesson 4 How Do Animals Change?

If possible, invite a student or parent to bring a baby animal to class for students to observe. Have students discuss how much the animal can do for itself and how it will change as it grows older. After students read the lesson, prompt a discussion about how all animals have a life cycle that repeats generation after generation.

Answers page 31: A. 1. True 2. False 3. True 4. False 5. True B. 4, 2, 1, 3 C. 2, 4, 3, 1 D. Students should say that all three start as eggs and grow into adults that are able to reproduce. Fish and birds develop in eggs outside their mothers' bodies, but rabbits develop from eggs inside. Rabbits and birds need to be fed by their parents after they are born, but fish do not need their parents.

Lesson 5 How Do People Grow and Change?

Before reading the lesson, engage students in a discussion about ways they have changed since they were born. Point out that the human life cycle is very similar to that of many animals. When students have read the lesson, have them name animals that have life cycles similar and dissimilar to that of humans. (similar: horses, dogs, monkeys; dissimilar: birds, insects, frogs)

Answers page 33: A. 1. mammals 2. inside 3. babies 4. adults 5. grow B. Answers will vary. Students might say that: 1. Babies learn many things very quickly. 2. Children grow at different speeds. 3. Adults are able to reproduce. C. Answers will vary, but students will probably recognize that they are children.

Lesson 6 What Are Characteristics?

Write the terms *inherited* and *learned* on the chalkboard. As students read the text, have them name examples of each type of characteristic.

Answers page 35: A. 1. a hard exoskeleton 2. inherit from 3. learned B. 1. learned 2. inherited 3. learned 4. inherited 5. inherited C. 1. Answers will vary, but should include an inherited characteristic. For example: A child can inherit red hair. 2. Answers will vary, but should include something the student has learned. For example: I learned how to in-line skate.

Hands-On Activity *page 36* Students will engage in the process skill of observing as they watch the fish and see how they respond to food. Have students make the charts before they begin observing the fish. Check the completed charts for accuracy, completeness, and attention to detail. This activity can be modified for use with an ant colony or other animals, such as birds, outside the classroom. Be sure that students observe for at least 15 minutes in order to notice changes in behavior.

Answers: 1. The animals get food from the fish food. Some animals may eat algae growing in the fish tank. They get water from the water in the tank. 2. The animals get oxygen from the water. (Students might notice that the fish seem to be breathing.) 3. Answers will vary. Students might say that they saw a fish eating food that had floated to the bottom. The fish picked up pebbles and then spit them out as it ate.

Blackline Masters for Chapter 2:

Problem Solving Skills, page 28; Chapter Review, page 35; Letter to Family (English), page 53; Letter to Family (Spanish), page 54

"What Is It?" *Answer:* exoskeleton

Chapter Test *page 37*

Answers: 1. B 2. B 3. A 4. D 5. D 6. B 7. C 8. C 9. D 10. A

After Reading the Chapter

Geography Provide students with a map of the world they can write on. Have students choose three animals and use references to locate where each animal lives. Students can then write the name of the animal in appropriate locations on the map.

Writing Invite students to write a story. Have them make the main character a young animal that is learning how to survive. Tell them that the story must be from the animal's point of view, describing what it is like to develop learned characteristics.

Chapter Summary Humans use their senses of sight, hearing, taste, smell, and touch to learn about the world. The sense organs—eyes, ears, nose, tongue, and skin—contain receptor cells that send signals to the brain about the outside world. All of the senses need protection. It is very important to take good care of them.

Chapter Objectives Students will learn to
- identify the senses and the nervous system.
- understand how the eyes work.
- explain the parts of the ears and how they work.
- understand how the senses of taste and smell work.
- identify the receptor cells used in the sense of touch.
- identify ways to protect the sense organs.

Vocabulary

sight, p. 40	cones, p. 42
hearing, p. 40	optic nerve, p. 42
smell, p. 40	outer ear, p. 44
taste, p. 40	middle ear, p. 44
touch, p. 40	inner ear, p. 44
receptor cells, p. 40	eardrum, p. 44
sense organs, p. 40	cochlea, p. 44
nerve cells, p. 40	taste buds, p. 46
nervous system, p. 40	odors, p. 46
pupil, p. 42	olfactory cells, p. 46
iris, p. 42	pressure receptor cells,
lens, p. 42	p. 48
retina, p. 42	prescription drugs, p. 50
rods, p. 42	

Vocabulary Activity Have students work in small groups and write sentences using the vocabulary words. When students have finished writing, ask for volunteers to read their sentences aloud and discuss the meaning of the vocabulary words.

Before Reading the Chapter Ask students to volunteer answers to the "What Is It?" riddle in the Chapter Opener. Then, have students close their eyes. Make a variety of sounds and ask them to listen to and identify each one. (You might whistle, crumple a piece of paper, pour water from one container into another, or drop five pencils onto the floor.) Then, ask students to discuss how they were able to identify the sounds. Lead students to realize that sound waves traveled through the air, were received by the sense organs (the ears), and were then recognized by the brain.

Lesson 1 How Can You Learn About the World?
Before reading the lesson, encourage students to sit quietly for a few minutes and focus on each of their senses. Ask them to pay attention to the sensations they are experiencing. Prompt a discussion about how life would be different without any one of the sense organs.

Answers page 41: A. 1. smell, and touch 2. receptor cells 3. sense organs 4. brain 5. nervous system B. 3, 1, 2 C. Answers will vary. Students might answer: If I smelled smoke, my brain would warn me that there could be a fire nearby. If I smelled a skunk, my brain would warn me that there could be a skunk nearby. Other answers might involve gas leaks or food burning on the stove or in the oven.

Lesson 2 How Do the Eyes Work?
When students have read the lesson, have them work in small groups to observe how the pupil of the eye adjusts to light conditions. Ask one student in each group to hold a flashlight. Have the other students in the group observe the size of that person's pupils. Then, ask the student to shine the light into his or her own eyes briefly. The students who are observing should discuss what they see. (The pupils will quickly become smaller, then gradually will grow larger.)

Answers page 43: A. 1. lens 2. pupil 3. iris 4. less 5. light 6. receptor B. 1. both 2. rods 3. cones C. Answers will vary. Students might say that the retina or rods on the retina may not work well. The rods are the cells that sense dim light. The retina or lens might also be damaged.

Lesson 3 How Do the Ears Work?

After students have read the lesson, have them draw their own diagram of the outer, middle, and inner ear. Ask students to include a source of sound in their diagrams. Then, write captions explaining the steps between the time a sound occurs and the time it is heard. Some students may wish to work together to make a large diagram that could be displayed in the classroom.

Answers page 45: A. 1. False 2. False 3. True B. 1. inner 2. receptor cells 3. brain C. 1. inner ear 2. middle ear 3. outer ear D. Louder sounds make more hairs in the cochlea move. Softer sounds make fewer hairs move.

Lesson 4 How Do Taste and Smell Work?

Bring a variety of items to class. These could include a flower, peppermint tea, garlic, an orange slice, cocoa, or sage. Have students close their eyes and sniff each item. Then, have students try to identify the items. Record and discuss their responses.

Answers page 47: A. 1. tongue 2. taste buds 3. salty 4. odors 5. olfactory cells 6. taste B. 1. False 2. False 3. True C. Answers will vary. Students might say that it can help you know when food is spoiled and not safe to eat.

Lesson 5 What Is Touch?

Before students read the lesson, have them exert different amounts of pressure on the skin of their palms. Ask them to describe the sensations. Repeat the activity after students have read the lesson. Ask students to explain why they feel different sensations. Help them recognize that each time they feel the sensation of touch, different receptor cells have sent signals through the nervous system to the brain. Ask them why they think there are many receptor cells in the fingertips. (Possible answer: Because we use our fingertips for many delicate tasks.)

Answers page 49: A. cold, heat, pressure, deep pressure, pain B. 1. No 2. No 3. Yes 4. No 5. Yes C. She's testing the milk to make sure it's not too hot or too cold. The inside of her wrist has many receptor cells, so it's a good place to test the temperature of the milk.

Lesson 6 How Can You Protect Your Senses?

Before assigning the reading, have students discuss why their senses are important. After students have read the lesson, emphasize that it is possible to damage one of the senses without realizing it. Explain that, for example, long exposure to loud music, particularly through headphones, can cause hearing loss many years later.

Answers page 51: A. 1. healthy 2. hearing 3. signals 4. when the doctor says you should B. 1. Yes 2. Yes 3. Yes 4. No 5. No C. Answers will vary, but students might say that the eardrum or the bones in the inner ear might be damaged by loud noises.

Hands-On Activity *page 52*

Students will engage in the process skill of observing as they touch different objects. Before conducting this activity, prepare four paper bags with different objects in each. Objects could include: erasers, pieces of cloth, metal cups or spoons, and other classroom objects. After students have completed the activity, have them talk about how they were able to recognize objects.

Answers: 1. Answers will vary, but should include size. 2. Answers will vary. Students might answer: My sense of hearing could tell me what something sounded like when it was shaken.

Blackline Masters for Chapter 3:

Problem Solving Skills, page 29; Chapter Review, page 36; Letter to Family (English), page 55; Letter to Family (Spanish), page 56

"What Is It?" *Answer:* cochlea

Chapter Test *page 53*

Answers: 1. B 2. B 3. A 4. D 5. B 6. C 7. C 8. B 9. C 10. D

After Reading the Chapter

Music Have students work in small groups and write a song about some or all of their senses. Suggest that they draw on information from the chapter as they write. Students can write the melody and lyrics or write new lyrics that go with a song they already know. Have students share their songs with the class.

Writing Invite students to write a story. Have them create a character who has an extraordinary sense of smell, sight, or hearing. Encourage students to jot down ideas about how life would be different with this powerful sense. Then, have them write a story in which this heightened sense plays an important part.

Unit Summary Earth is an ever-changing planet. All living things exist in ecosystems where they exchange energy in food chains. Landforms are changed by natural forces and by people. Earth is one of nine planets orbiting a sun, and the only planet that sustains life as we know it. People need to keep the planet clean and safe for all living things.

Before Reading the Unit Point out that everything on Earth changes. Ask students if they can think of any exceptions. Ask them, which things grow and die? Which things change quickly and which things change slowly? Which changes are predictable? Ask students to give examples of how some of these changes affect people and other living things. Tell students that they will learn more about the processes of living things, Earth's landforms, and our solar system in Unit 2.

Unit Performance Project

Setup and Presentation Page 48 in this Teacher's Guide is a reproducible project that focuses on our changing planet. Present the project after you have studied ecosystems (Chapter 4). As you present the project, advise students to choose a site that includes both plant and animal life. The animal life will most likely be insects. Remind students to make several visits to the site and to write their observations in a log.

Evaluation A satisfactory project should include some notes about plant and animal interactions, a visual representation of an observation, or an explanation of the food web.

A good project should include substantial notes about plant and animal interactions, including visual representation of some observations, and explanations of the food web. The food web should reflect the notes.

An outstanding project should include detailed, accurate notes about plant and animal interactions, a visual representation of the results of numerous observations, and detailed explanations for the relationships that exist in the food web. The food web should reflect the notes in virtually every aspect.

There is a rubric on page 50 in this Teacher's Guide that will assist students in evaluating their own work on the unit performance project.

Careers Feature

Page 104 of the student text offers students a glimpse into these careers: wildlife conservationist, oceanographer, and astronomer. Explain that professionals in each of these fields attend four years of college after high school, specializing in biology, zoology, earth science, chemistry, or physics. These scientists often continue studying in graduate school, focusing on a particular issue or questions in their field. For example, a wildlife conservationist might study stream restoration in a particular river, an oceanographer might work as an intern on an ocean survey, and an astronomer might spend several years analyzing photographs sent back from the Hubbell telescope. Suggest students choose one of the fields to research. Have them talk to people in the field, or read articles on the Internet or in recent periodicals to learn about recent developments in the field. Ask them to write a brief report on the topic.

Unit Test The Blackline Master for Unit 2 Test is on page 42 of the Teacher's Guide. The test is in the standardized test format to provide students with practice in taking standardized tests. The unit test content focuses on ecosystems, landforms and rocks, and astronomers and the solar system. The test also covers ideas about protecting life on Earth.

Answers: 1. B 2. B 3. A 4. D 5. D 6. B 7. C 8. C 9. D 10. A

After Reading the Unit Engage students in a discussion about how they can use the information they learned in this unit in their everyday lives. Ask them to consider what they have learned about natural and human-made changes affecting life on Earth. Ask how this knowledge has changed the way they think about nature and the environment, and how it might change their behavior.

Chapter Summary Every living thing on Earth is part of an ecosystem—a community where plants, animals, and nonliving things exchange energy. In every ecosystem, living things compete for resources, and there is constant change. Most changes are natural and healthy. However, some changes made by people can harm or destroy an ecosystem. People can protect ecosystems by following the three Rs: reduce, reuse, and recycle.

Chapter Objectives Students will learn to
- define the word *ecosystem*.
- understand how energy is exchanged in an ecosystem.
- describe how living things compete in an ecosystem.
- understand that ecosystems change naturally.
- explain how people change ecosystems.
- identify ways to protect ecosystems.

Vocabulary

ecosystem, p. 58	compete, p. 62
nonliving, p. 58	competition, p. 62
producers, p. 60	extinct, p. 64
consumers, p. 60	pollution, p. 66
herbivores, p. 60	nature preserves, p. 68
carnivores, p. 60	reduce, p. 68
omnivores, p. 60	reuse, p. 68
decomposers, p. 60	recycle, p. 68
food chain, p. 60	

Vocabulary Activity Explain that prefixes such as *eco-, omni-, carni-, com-,* and *re-* can be keys for understanding the meaning of words. Show students how to look up a prefix in the dictionary. Have students work in groups of four to look up four vocabulary words in the dictionary. Have groups explain which words are formed by roots and prefixes and discuss the meaning of the words.

Before Reading the Chapter Ask students to volunteer answers to the "What Is It?" riddle in the Chapter Opener. Then, ask students to describe a nature preserve they may have visited. If possible, visit and then describe one near your school. On the chalkboard, list sights and sounds students have experienced while at the preserve.

Lesson 1 What Is an Ecosystem?
After reading the lesson, discuss how different ecosystems support living things. Ask students to tell how an ocean ecosystem and a forest ecosystem are different. (An ocean ecosystem contains saltwater, sand, fish, crabs, seaweed, and whales; a forest ecosystem contains soil, freshwater, air, trees, squirrels, and birds.) Ask how they are alike. (They are both suitable homes for living things.)
    Answers page 59: A. 1. True 2. True 3. False 4. True B. living things—fox, rabbit, trees, bushes; nonliving things—stream, soil, rock, air (also sunlight) C. Answers will vary, but students should indicate that the desert ecosystem would not provide the robin what it needs to survive.

Lesson 2 What Lives in an Ecosystem?
Before reading the lesson, invite students to create a bulletin board showing the web of life. Have them cut magazine photographs of animals and plants and draw pictures of living things. After the lesson, help students post the illustrations and label them using vocabulary words. Direct students to use string or draw arrows from picture to picture to show the movement of energy through the food chain.
    Answers page 61: A. 1. producers 2. consumers 3. decomposers 4. food chain B. producers—berry bush, other plants, trees; consumers—mouse, snake, bird C. Animals that the bird eats, like mice, need plants to live. Without plants, the bird would have no food.

Lesson 3 How Do Living Things Compete?
As you discuss the lesson, invite volunteers to consider one plant or animal that lives in an ecosystem nearby. Ask students to name two things that every living thing needs to survive. Ask how the plant or animal competes with other living things in the ecosystem.

Answers page 63: A. 1. True 2. True 3. False 4. True B. 1. Plants compete for water and sunlight. 2. Animals compete for food, a place to live, water, and to be the leader of their group. C. 1. The ducks are competing for the insect. 2. A duck will win by getting to the insect first.

Lesson 4 How Do Ecosystems Change?
Illustrate ways in which ecosystems change rapidly by showing students photographs of natural disasters. Ask students to describe the changes they observe. If possible, include some photographs of ecosystems renewing themselves after a fire or flood.
    Answers page 65: A. 1. True 2. True 3. False 4. False 5. False B. 1. Fast 2. Fast 3. Fast 4. Slow 5. Slow 6. Fast C. Answers will vary, but students might mention that the lava might cover and kill all of the plants.

Lesson 5 How Do People Change Ecosystems?
After students read the lesson, point out that people change distant ecosystems without being aware of it. For example, the paper they use in school may come from a forest in another state. Ask students to offer examples of how people have changed ecosystems near you. Encourage students to learn how people in your community have helped restore ecosystems.
    Answers page 67: A. 1. changes 2. scare 3. pollution 4. cars 5. plant B. Sample answers: 1. People have cut down trees. 2. People have built roads and buildings. 3. People have added pollution. C. Answers will vary, but students might mention that larger fish and other animals, such as turtles and birds, could also die because they used to eat the small fish.

Lesson 6 How Can People Protect Ecosystems?
To close the lesson, help students list ways to help protect ecosystems. Under the headings *reduce, reuse,* and *recycle,* suggest that students list responsible actions that will make a difference both in the classroom and at home.
    Answers page 69: A. 1. A nature preserve is a special park where nature is left alone. 2. People make nature preserves to protect ecosystems. 3. The three Rs stand for *reduce, reuse,* and *recycle.* 4. The three Rs help ecosystems by making less pollution. B. 1. recycle 2. reuse 3. reduce C. Answers will vary, but

students might mention that people like nature and want to see wildlife protected from extinction.

Hands-On Activity *page 70* Students will engage in the process skill of observing as they watch an ecosystem in action. Select an appropriate area in advance. Any grassy area near the school will likely have insect life. Rocks and branches provide interesting habitats. Invite students to sketch as they observe. Note: You may want to remind students that all creatures in the ecosystem are to be respected. Discourage the misuse of the hand lens.
    Answers: 1. Answers will vary, but students should mention living things, such as worms, ants, and grass, and nonliving things, such as dead grass, dirt, and rocks they may find. 2. Answers will vary, but students should list the activities they saw, such as ants walking around and carrying leaves and other things. 3. Answers will vary, but students should mention what one living thing needed to stay alive. For example, the ants used plants for food and dirt for their home. They breathed the air.

Blackline Masters for Chapter 4:
Problem Solving Skills, page 30; Chapter Review, page 37; Letter to Family (English), page 57; Letter to Family (Spanish), page 58

"What Is It?" *Answer:* omnivore

Chapter Test *page 71*
    Answers: 1. C 2. D 3. A 4. C 5. A 6. A 7. D 8. C 9. A 10. B

After Reading the Chapter
Writing Ask students to write poems about their experiences in nature and what they learned about ecosystems. Some students may want to enter the annual National Environmental Poetry Contest for Students, *River of Words.* For guidelines, contact the International Rivers Network, 1847 Berkeley Way, Berkeley, CA 94703; phone, (510) 848-1155.
Social Studies Help students plan an ecosystem protection project. Students may want to improve recycling programs in your school, make a poster, or talk to other classes about reducing lunchtime waste.

Chapter Summary Earth's landforms include mountains, hills, plateaus, and plains that change constantly. Most changes are slow and steady, due to erosion by weather and wind. Because molten rock exists beneath Earth's crust, the crust is sometimes changed quickly by volcanoes or earthquakes. Rocks on the crust— igneous, sedimentary, and metamorphic—are formed by heat and pressure. There are landforms even under the ocean. There is also oil under the ocean floor that people use for fuel.

Chapter Objectives Students will learn to
• name and describe Earth's landforms.
• understand how erosion and weathering change landforms.
• describe how volcanoes and earthquakes change landforms.
• understand how rocks are formed.
• identify the landforms found under the ocean's surface.
• explain how people use and affect the ocean.

Vocabulary

landforms, p. 74	erupt, p. 78
mountain, p. 74	igneous, p. 80
hill, p. 74	sedimentary, p. 80
plateau, p. 74	metamorphic, p. 80
plain, p. 74	ocean floor, p. 82
weathering, p. 76	continental shelf, p. 82
erosion, p. 76	open ocean, p. 82
layers, p. 78	abyss, p. 82
crust, p. 78	ocean currents, p. 82
volcano, p. 78	ships, p. 84
earthquakes, p. 78	tankers, p. 84
plates, p. 78	oil spill, p. 84
landslide, p. 78	

Vocabulary Activity Help students create a chalkboard drawing illustrating the vocabulary words. Draw silhouettes of the landforms and ask volunteers to label them. Throughout the chapter, invite students to add cartoons illustrating concepts like erosion, landslide, and oil spill.

Before Reading the Chapter Ask students to volunteer answers to the "What Is It?" riddle in the Chapter Opener. Then, if possible, take a walk outside and point out local landforms to the students. (You may also want to collect specimens of rock for the discussion in Lesson 4.) Ask students to compare the landforms and rocks in your area to those they have seen in other places.

Lesson 1 What Are Landforms?
Organize the students into groups of four to draw landform maps. Tell three groups to map different regions of your neighborhood, based on their own observations. Ask the other groups to create state maps. Invite students to share their completed maps.
Answers page 75: A. 1. plain—This is a low, flat, or rolling landform that can be covered with grass. 2. mountain—This is the highest landform with few flat places. 3. plateau— This landform is also high, but it is very flat. 4. hill—This landform usually has a rounded shape.
B. 1. landform 2. mountain 3. trees 4. plain 5. buffalo C. You would be on a mountain. It would not be a plain or a plateau, because they are both flat. It would not be a hill because it has steep slopes.

Lesson 2 How Do Landforms Change Slowly?
Use photographs or maps from a state geologic service or park system to illustrate gradual landform changes. After the lesson, take students to a nearby body of water. Point out signs of change along the streambed or beach. Ask if students have noticed changes here over seasons or during longer periods of time. Plan a return trip to make a record of any changes.
Answers page 77: A. 1. False 2. True 3. False 4. True 5. False B. 1. weathering 2. landform 3. wind 4. pieces of rock 5. very slowly C. Tiny pieces of rock that were in the water hit the side of the rock. In time, the tiny pieces took away parts of the rock and made it smooth.

Lesson 3 How Do Landforms Change Quickly?
Show students photographs of dramatic changes in landforms made by volcanoes, earthquakes, and landslides. Ask students to describe their observations.

Answers page 79: A. 1. quickly 2. crust
3. hot B. 1. volcano 2. landform 3. move
4. earthquake C. There has been an earthquake
that made the dishes rattle. It has also caused a
landslide that made a pile of rocks and soil
in your neighbor's yard.

Lesson 4 How Do Rocks Form and Change?
Invite a geologist to speak to the class. Or bring
rock collections found in hobby shops or science supply catalogues to class. Encourage
students to use field guides to identify the rocks
and the processes that made them.

Answers page 81: A. 1. igneous 2. pressed
3. earthquakes 4. metamorphic 5. sedimentary
B. 1. False 2. False 3. True 4. True 5. False
C. Answers will vary. Students should say that
they found sedimentary rock. They might
explain that their yards may have once been
the bottom of an ocean. Seashells and bits of
rock on the ocean bottom were pressed together
to form sedimentary rock.

Lesson 5 What Is the Ocean Like?
You may want to present a videotape that
provides an underwater view of ocean-bottom
landforms. You may also want to encourage
students to build models of ocean-bottom
landforms.

Answers page 83: A. 1. three-quarters
2. abyss 3. ocean currents B. 1. True 2. False
3. True C. 1. Ocean currents are rivers of moving ocean water. 2. The abyss is the deepest part
of the ocean. 3. The ocean floor is the bottom of
the ocean. 4. The continental shelf is the part of
the ocean floor closest to land. D. Ocean plants
can only live near the surface, so the
plant-eaters must live there. Animals that eat
the plant-eaters must also live there.

Lesson 6 How Do People Affect the Ocean?
Lead a discussion about taking care of the
ocean. Ask students to research and report on
overfishing and ocean pollution. Guide
students to understand that the responsibility
for pollution is shared by large companies and
everyone who uses oil, eats fish, and throws
away garbage. Ask students to think of actions
they might take to protect the ocean.

Answers page 85: A. 1. food 2. tanker 3. oil
spill 4. pollution 5. clean B. 1. under the ocean

floor 2. food 3. garbage C. Answers will vary,
but students might say that the ocean is like a
highway because people can travel on it. Ships
with goods that people need also travel on the
ocean like trucks travel on roads on land.

Hands-On Activity *page 86* Students will
engage in the process skills of observing and
modeling erosion. For this activity, provide
large plastic trays, such as flats found at plant
stores. Also provide several containers for
pouring water, including a watering can with a
sprinkling spout, and a small fan.

Allow students to rebuild their landforms
and repeat the activities several times.
Encourage them to experiment with different
kinds of "weather" by varying the amount,
speed, and direction of the "wind" and "rain."
Guide them to make connections between this
activity and real world weathering and erosion.

Answers: 1. Answers will vary. Students
might say that the water made a river in the plain.
The water washed away the side of the mountain.
2. Answers will vary. Students might say that the
wind did not change the mountain. The wind
made little hills in the plain. 3. No, it blew the dry
sand, but it did not blow the wet sand.

Blackline Masters for Chapter 5:
Problem Solving Skills, page 31; Chapter
Review, page 38; Letter to Family (English),
page 59; Letter to Family (Spanish), page 60

"What Is It?" *Answer:* weathering

Chapter Test *page 87*
Answers: 1. D 2. B 3. C 4. A 5. C 6. D 7. B
8. C 9. A 10. D

After Reading the Chapter
Art Help students make a papier-mâché map
of your state, showing the major landforms.
Paint the map and label landforms with names
and elevations.
Mathematics Provide an atlas and ask students
to find the highest altitude on Earth and the
lowest depth of the ocean floor. Have them select
ten more locations to research. Then help them
draw a bar graph of the varying altitudes, using
a scale of one-fourth inch for every 4000 feet.

Chapter Summary We live on Earth, one of nine planets that orbit the sun. Our planet has one orbiting moon. In our solar system, the inner planets—those closest to the sun—are Mercury, Venus, Earth, and Mars. The outer planets are Jupiter, Saturn, Uranus, Neptune, and Pluto. There are other solid objects moving in our solar system—comets, asteroids, and meteors.

Chapter Objectives Students will learn to
- name and describe the functions of astronomers' tools.
- understand how planets orbit the sun.
- explain the moon's relationship to Earth.
- identify and describe other planets in our solar system.
- distinguish differences and similarities among comets, asteroids, and meteoroids.

Vocabulary

astronomers, p. 90	Mercury, p. 96
optical telescope, p. 90	Venus, p. 96
radio telescope, p. 90	Earth, p. 96
space probe, p. 90	Mars, p. 96
solar system, p. 92	outer planets, p. 98
orbit, p. 92	Jupiter, p. 98
planets, p. 92	Saturn, p. 98
gravity, p. 92	Uranus, p. 98
year, p. 92	Neptune, p. 98
rotates, p. 92	Pluto, p. 98
day, p. 92	comets, p. 100
moon, p. 94	asteroids, p. 100
phases, p. 94	asteroid belt, p. 100
full moon, p. 94	minor planets, p. 100
crescent moon, p. 94	meteor, p. 100
astronauts, p. 94	meteoroids, p. 100
craters, p. 94	meteorite, p. 100
inner planets, p. 96	meteor shower, p. 100

Vocabulary Activity Write each vocabulary word once on each of five separate small sheets

of paper. Place all of the written words in a paper bag. Ask students to draw six words and use these words in a story about space exploration. Students can then read their stories aloud.

Before Reading the Chapter Ask students to volunteer answers to the "What Is It?" riddle in the Chapter Opener. Then, discuss the night sky. Ask students if they have seen planets. Ask if they have noticed changes in star patterns at different times of the night or year. Have students describe what they might think the stars were if they knew nothing at all about them.

Lesson 1 What Tools Do Astronomers Use?
Show students photographs of our solar system. Science magazines will have photographs, for example, of the surface of Mars and Saturn's rings. Be sure students understand that technology gives us a new view of space. Point out the advantages of uncrewed telescopes and probes.
Answers page 91: A. 1. √ 3. √ 5. √ B. 1. True 2. False 3. False 4. True C. Answers will vary, but students should explain the basic difference between the two types of telescopes. For example, optical telescopes collect light and you look through them. Radio telescopes pick up radio waves and you don't look through them. D. Answers will vary. You might discuss with students that it is easier and cheaper to send probes to closer objects, such as the moon, than to faraway objects, such as the outer planets.

Lesson 2 What Is Our Solar System?
Demonstrate how seasons result from Earth's orbit. Place a basketball in the center of the room to represent the sun. Explain that rotating Earth is tilted, and demonstrate this with a classroom globe. Walk the globe in an orbit around the basketball, always tilting it in the same direction. Point out that the southern and northern hemispheres get more direct light from the sun at opposite times of the year, creating opposite seasons.
Answers page 93: A. 1. solar system—sun and everything that circles it 2. planet—large object that circles the sun 3. orbit—to circle the sun or other object 4. gravity—force that pulls objects to each other 5. year—time it takes Earth

to circle the sun once 6. rotate—to spin like a top 7. day—time it takes Earth to spin around once B. 1. the sun 2. nine 3. day 4. year
C. Earth rotates about 365 times in one year.

Lesson 3 What Is the Moon?
Demonstrate the moon's phases. Darken the classroom. Place a flashlight to represent sunlight, a basketball to represent Earth, and a baseball to represent the moon, in a row. Shine the flashlight toward the baseball. The baseball should be between the flashlight and the basketball. Move the baseball in orbit around the basketball. Explain that if the baseball were the moon, we would see only the part of the moon that reflects the sun's light.

Answers page 95: A. 1. False 2. True
3. False 4. False 5. True B. 1. month 2. phases
3. full 4. crescent 5. craters C. Answers will vary. Students might mention that craters on the moon can last millions of years because there is no air or running water to cause weathering or erosion on the moon's surface.

Lesson 4 What Are the Inner Planets?
Ask students to share stories about Martians or other space people from books they've read or movies they've seen. Be sure they understand that astronomers have not detected signs of life on other planets in our solar system.

Answers page 97: A. 3, 1, 4, 2 B. 1. land-forms 2. Mercury 3. Venus 4. moons
C. 1. Mercury 2. Venus 3. Earth 4. Mars
D. Answers will vary. Students might say that people can only breathe the air on Earth because the other inner planets have different kinds of atmospheres. For example, Mercury's atmosphere is very thin. Venus is covered with an atmosphere of thick, yellowish clouds of acid.

Lesson 5 What Are the Outer Planets?
Create a solar system bulletin board. Ask students to draw the planets and their moons from photographs. Have groups of students write descriptive captions for each planet. Post captioned drawings, in order, orbiting the sun.

Answers page 99: A. 3, 1, 5, 4, 2
B. 1. Jupiter 2. Saturn 3. Uranus 4. Neptune
5. Pluto C. 1. False 2. True 3. True D. Pluto is the coldest planet because it is so far from the sun.

Lesson 6 What Are Comets, Asteroids, and Meteoroids?
Before reading, ask students if they have seen shooting stars and if they saw the comet Hale-Bopp in 1997. Have students share information about comets and shooting stars, and list any questions they may have. During the lesson, discuss the answers to their questions.

Answers page 101: A. 1. meteor—in Earth's atmosphere 2. meteorite—on the surface of Earth
3. meteoroid—in outer space B. 1. ovals 2. comets
3. gases 4. asteroids 5. asteroid belt C. Answers will vary. Students might mention that asteroids are like planets because they orbit the sun.

Hands-On Activity *page 102* Students will engage in the process skill of modeling as they build a model of the solar system. To prepare for the activity, bring in balloons that will inflate to a diameter of 16 inches. You can also substitute paper bags stuffed with packing peanuts for the outer planets or have students make papier-mâché planets if there is time.

Note: Explain that the model is accurate in terms of the relative sizes of the planets, not in terms of their relative distances to the sun.

Answers: 1. The inner planets and the outer planets are all round. They all orbit the sun. The inner planets are smaller than all of the outer planets except Pluto. The inner planets and the outer planets are made of different materials.
2. Venus is about the same size as Earth.

Blackline Masters for Chapter 6:
Problem Solving Skills, page 32; Chapter Review, page 39; Letter to Family (English), page 61; Letter to Family (Spanish), page 62

"What Is It?" *Answer:* Mars

Chapter Test *page 103*
Answers: 1. D 2. B 3. C 4. B 5. C 6. C 7. A
8. B 9. A 10. C

After Reading the Chapter
Geography Ask students to write researched reports on the geography of the moon and Mars. Encourage them to describe how landforms on Mars and the moon compare to those found on Earth.

Unit Summary Energy comes in many forms, including light, sound, and electricity. White light contains many colors. When objects vibrate, they create sound. Magnets push or pull other magnets and metal objects. Electricity is used for light, heat, sound, and a number of other purposes.

Before Reading the Unit Have students think of examples of sound and light. Point out that these, like electricity, are forms of energy. Then ask students to clap their hands. Have them explain where the energy came from for these sounds. Explain that the students vibrated the air by clapping their hands and that the energy came from their bodies.

Unit Performance Project

Setup and Presentation Page 49 in the Teacher's Guide is a reproducible project that focuses on sound. Before you present the project, you may wish to engage students in a short discussion about how to draw a number line. Make sure they know how to mark off equal intervals on the number line and that they label the line correctly. Present the project to students after they have learned about sound. (Chapter 7, Lesson 3)

Evaluation A satisfactory project should include a chart and some notes about sounds that the student heard. The chart should be completed with the names of at least a few sound-making objects.

A good project should include fairly detailed notes about sounds that the student heard. The chart should be completed with the names of several sound-making objects.

An outstanding project should include detailed, accurate notes about sounds that the student heard. The chart should be completed with the names of a large number of sound-making objects, and be neat and easy to read.

There is a rubric on page 50 in this Teacher's Guide that will assist students in evaluating their own work on the unit performance project.

Careers Feature

Page 122 of the student text offers a glimpse into these careers: photographer, optical engineer, and lens grinder. Explain that all of these careers involve light and electricity in some form. Point out to students that people in these careers generally receive their training either on the job or in schools.

Students interested in these careers should be encouraged to take science classes, particularly physics, as well as classes in art, math, and computer science. Ask students to think of other qualifications a photographer or an engineer might need. (mechanical skills, computer skills, critical thinking skills, working well with other people) You might suggest that students find out more about one of these careers. They can use the Internet or recent periodicals. Encourage them to learn about developments in the field that have occurred during the past year. Then, have them write a brief summary of what they have learned.

Unit Test The Blackline Master for Unit 3 Test is on page 43 of the Teacher's Guide. The test is in the standardized test format to provide students with practice in taking standardized tests. The unit test content focuses on light, sound, magnets, and electricity.

Answers: 1. D 2. C 3. B 4. D 5. B 6. A 7. C 8. A 9. D 10. B

After Reading the Unit Ask students to discuss how they can use information about light, sound, magnets, and electricity in their daily lives. How does understanding about the colors in light change their ideas about the colors they see? Ask students to explain how they might use the information they've learned about sound to understand various musical instruments. Write their ideas on the chalkboard.

Chapter Summary Energy comes in many forms, including light. White light is made up of many colors mixed together. A prism breaks light into colors. Light travels in a straight line until it is reflected, absorbed, or refracted. When objects vibrate, they create sound. Sound travels in waves. A magnet is an object that pulls or pushes other magnets or pieces of metal. All magnets have two poles. Electricity is a form of energy that is used for light, heat, sound, and many other purposes. The circle that electricity travels in is called a circuit.

Chapter Objectives Students will learn to
- understand light and color.
- identify reflected, absorbed, and refracted light.
- understand how we hear sound.
- explain magnetism and how a magnet operates.
- list ways that we use electricity.
- understand electricity and circuits.

Vocabulary

white light, p. 108	magnet, p. 114
prism, p. 108	magnetism, p. 114
reflected, p. 110	poles, p. 114
absorbed, p. 110	north, p. 114
refracted, p. 110	south, p. 114
vibrates, p. 112	electricity, p. 116
sound wave, p. 112	circuit, p. 118
pitch, p. 112	batteries, p. 118
volume, p. 112	power plant, p. 118

Vocabulary Activity Have students create a semantic word map for each of the following words: *light, sound, magnetism, electricity*. Then, have them group each of the other vocabulary words in the appropriate place and discuss their meanings with a partner. (*light*: white light, prism, reflected, absorbed, refracted; *sound*: vibrates, sound wave, pitch, volume; *magnetism*: magnet, poles, north, south; *electricity*: circuit, batteries, power plant)

Before Reading the Chapter Ask students to volunteer answers to the "What Is It?" riddle in the Chapter Opener. Then, write the word *energy* on the chalkboard. Ask students to brainstorm as many ideas as possible about energy. Record their responses. Elicit the ideas that energy is everywhere and constantly changing form, and without it, there would be no sun, no water, no fire, and no life. Point out that some of the most familiar forms of energy include light, heat, sound, and electricity.

Lesson 1 What Is Light?
Introduce the lesson by demonstrating what happens when light passes through a prism. You might also want to show how colors combine by covering three flashlights with layers of red, blue, and green cellophane respectively. Dim the lights and shine the red light on a piece of white paper. Then, shine the green on top of it to produce a yellow spot. Finally, shine the blue light on the yellow spot, which will create a nearly white light. The light will not be pure white because the cellophane colors used to make it are not exactly complementary.

Answers page 109: A. 1. White light can come from the sun or from a lightbulb. 2. A prism is a special piece of glass that spreads the colors of light. 3. A rainbow is made when raindrops act like a giant prism. B. 1. color 2. many colors mixed together 3. blue 4. bends 5. sunlight C. No, because we see just the part of the light that bounces back from something. If the white light didn't have red in it, there would be no red part of the light to bounce back.

Lesson 2 How Does Light Travel?
Explain that the movement of light can affect how buildings are constructed. Ask students to describe the ideal surface color and texture for a building in a very hot climate. Help students understand that they want the surface to reflect light in order to stay cool, which means a smooth, light-colored surface would work best.

Answers page 111: A. 1. reflected 2. absorbed 3. refracted B. 1. True 2. False 3. True 4. True 5. False 6. True C. A smooth, bright yellow marker would be better, because it will reflect light better than a rough, dark blue one.

Lesson 3 What Is Sound?

If possible, have a student bring a guitar to class. Allow students to gently pluck one of the strings and observe how it vibrates and then comes to rest. After students have read the lesson, initiate a discussion about how the vibrations of the string cause sound waves to travel through the air.

Answers page 113: A. 1. vibrations 2. through different things 3. sound wave 4. pitch 5. volume B. 4, 2, 1, 5, 3 C. The sound that the tiny bird makes sounds higher, because faster vibrations make higher sounds.

Lesson 4 What Is a Magnet?

After students have read the lesson, allow them to experiment with pairs of magnets. Point out that the north pole of a magnet will line up with Earth's magnetic north pole. Hang a bar magnet from a string to demonstrate this. Let it settle and be sure there are no metal objects nearby. Ask students to suggest how this principle is commonly used. (to make a compass)

Answers page 115: A. 1. True 2. False 3. True 4. True 5. False B. 1. pull toward 2. push away from C. You should put them so that the different poles of the magnets go together. The magnets will pull toward each other.

Lesson 5 How Is Electricity Used?

Have students read the first paragraph of the text. Then, have them imagine a day without electricity. Ask them to suggest how life would be different. Encourage them to think of items that would be hard to live without and items that might be less difficult to live without.

Answers page 117: A. 1. energy 2. more difficult 3. sound B. Answers will vary. Accept all reasonable answers. C. These jobs would have been much harder a hundred years ago. Electricity helps us do these jobs now by making washing machines, stoves, and heaters work.

Lesson 6 What Is a Circuit?

Before assigning the reading, demonstrate an electric circuit for the class. You can use a battery, two wires, and a small bulb (6 volt) or motor. Have students help set up the circuit. You may wish to add a switch to show how the circuit can be broken. Or, simply disconnect one of the wires. Prompt a discussion about why

the bulb or motor goes on and off. After the lesson, stress the idea that all electric current must be in a complete circuit to work.

Answers page 119: A. 1. travels 2. circuit 3. battery 4. power plant B. Students should draw a wire from the battery to the lightbulb to complete the electrical circuit. C. No, the lights and the stove wouldn't work. There would be no electricity, because the broken wires would break the circuit.

Hands-On Activity *page 120* Students will engage in the process skill of modeling as they make a telephone from paper cups and line. Provide students with needed materials. Do not substitute regular cotton string for floss or fishing line. String does not carry sound waves nearly as well. Students should find that the sound travels better when the line is held tight.

Answers: 1. Answers will vary. Students might mention that the sound vibrated along the line. 2. Answers will vary.

Blackline Masters for Chapter 7: Problem Solving Skills, page 33; Chapter Review, page 40; Letter to Family (English), page 63; Letter to Family (Spanish), page 64

"What Is It?" *Answer:* magnet

Chapter Test *page 121*
   Answers: 1. B 2. C 3. A 4. D 5. C 6. D 7. B 8. A 9. D 10. B

After Reading the Chapter

Music Provide students with plastic bottles that are the same size (the 1-liter size works well). Put different amounts of water in each bottle. Then, have small groups create music by blowing across the tops of their bottles. Encourage group members to listen to each other to make a song with a steady beat and parts that go together.

Social Studies Have students learn about the source of electricity in their community. Ask them to make a map showing their community and the location of its power source. Some maps may cover a large area. Students should indicate the type of power source and draw lines from it to their community.

CHAPTER 1

Name _____ Date _____

Problem Solving Skill

Making Inferences

Trees grow and change. Each year a tree grows, it adds a ring of growth. When a tree is cut, scientists can count the rings inside it to tell the age of the tree. The rings can tell scientists more than just the age of a tree. The rings also tell about the climate. For example, the size of rings (the space between lines) is larger in years when there is more rain because the tree grew more.

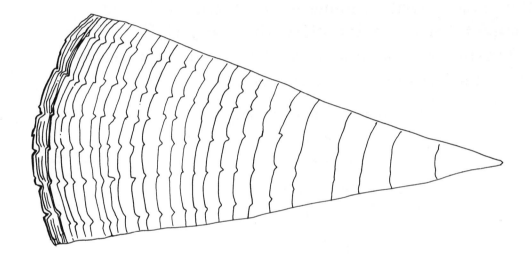

You are a scientist who is studying a very old village, where people lived more than 1,000 years ago. The people suddenly moved away from the village. You want to know why. You have found pieces of wood from shelters that these ancient people built. Look closely at the wood shown above. What do you see that could help you explain why the people left their village?

_____

_____

_____

_____

_____

Name _____   Date _____

Problem Solving Skill

Observing and Recording

Everyone has characteristics. Some characteristics are things we learn. Knowing how to swim is a learned characteristic. We inherit other characteristics, such as hair color, from our parents.

Think of five characteristics that you have inherited. The color of your eyes is one example. Draw the characteristics on the drawing of the person. Write a name for each characteristic. Connect the name to its characteristic with a line. Then, think of four characteristics you have learned. Use the four boxes to draw pictures that show the characteristics you have learned.

Inherited Characteristics

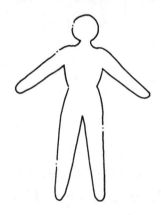

Learned Characteristics

Name _____ Date _____

Problem Solving Skill

Making Inferences

You are going to be a leader at *Camp Lotsafun,* a summer camp for six-year-old children. You want to be sure that they have a good time and stay healthy. Write a letter to the campers' parents to explain what kinds of things the children should bring to camp. Remember some problems at summer camp, like loud noises, hot summer sun, poison oak or ivy, campfires, and different kinds of accidents. Your letter should suggest ways that the children can have a great time and protect their sense organs.

Name _____ Date _____

Problem Solving Skill

Offer Solutions

You own all of the land you see in the picture. You also own a paper company. Your company has been in business a long time, but things are changing. You have cut most of the trees from part of your land. Now you have only a small supply of trees left, and you may lose your company.

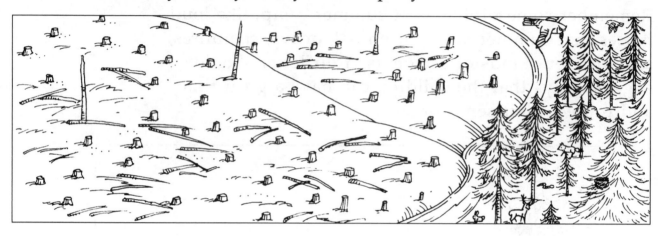

Write a business plan that will help you keep your land and your business for a long time.

New Business Plan
New Goals for My Company: To stay in business. To bring back the forest.

1. Some things I can't do anymore if I'm going to meet my goals:

_____

_____

2. Some things I'm going to do to help me meet my goals:

_____

_____

3. Ideas for new ways to make paper to help my company grow:

_____

_____

Problem Solving Skill

Making Predictions

Look closely at the picture.

1. What landforms do you see?

_____

_____

_____

2. Explain how you think these landforms might have formed.

_____

_____

_____

3. Describe how you think this land might look 100 years from now.

_____

_____

_____

Problem Solving Skill

Applying Information

Use a sundial to observe the sun's position in the sky for one full day.

Cut a round piece of cardboard. Make a hole in the middle of the cardboard circle. Put one end of a tall stick in the hole. Find an open space that receives full sunlight. Put your sundial there. Observe where the stick's shadow falls on the sundial. Mark the position of the shadow by writing the time of your observation. Return to the sundial each hour. Mark the position of the shadow each time.

Describe what you observe. Explain why this happens, using what you have learned about the motion of Earth as it turns on its axis.

_____

_____

_____

_____

_____

_____

_____

_____

_____

CHAPTER 7

Name _____ Date _____

Problem Solving Skill

Analyzing Information

You are on vacation with some friends. You and your friends take a hike in the woods. Rain begins to fall and fog forms. You lose the trail. You can't see the trail, but you know that there is a town one mile north and another town one mile south. The closest town east or west from where you are is more than ten miles away. You must find a way to the nearest town. You have some things with you that will help you.

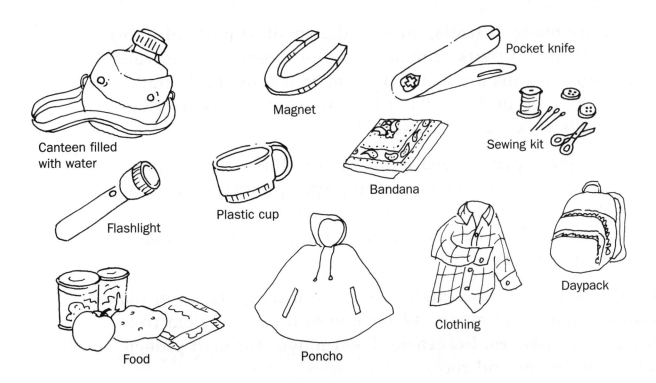

Canteen filled with water

Magnet

Pocket knife

Sewing kit

Bandana

Flashlight

Plastic cup

Clothing

Daypack

Food

Poncho

Look at the things in the picture. How can you use these things to find your way to the nearest town?

_____

_____

_____

_____

Focus on Science Level D

Name _____ Date _____

Chapter Review

Each of the following paragraphs tells about something you read in Chapter 1. Read each paragraph. Underline the word that makes each sentence correct.

Nearly all plants have three main parts—roots, stems, and leaves. Roots help keep plants in place and take in water from the soil. Stems hold plants up and carry water and **(light, food)** through the plant. Most of a plant's food is made in its **(leaves, seeds)**.

Plants are made of **(cells, atoms)**, the smallest parts of living things. Different parts of plants have different kinds of cells. For example, leaf cells are different from root cells. Each kind of cell has its own job to do. Cells of the same kind work together. These cells make **(bricks, tissues)**.

To make food, plants need light, carbon dioxide, and water. Plants use a process called **(chlorophyll, photosynthesis)** to make food. When plants make their food they give off **(light, oxygen)**. Plants are the only living things that make their own **(water, food)**.

Food, water, and other materials move through tubes in plants called xylem and phloem. Water moves through xylem from roots up to **(leaves, branches)**. Food moves through phloem to and from leaves and roots.

Plants react to their surroundings. Stems and leaves grow toward **(water, light)**. Roots grow **(down, up)** in the soil. Many plants lose their **(leaves, roots)** before winter comes. During hot, sunny days the flowers on some desert plants **(close, die)**.

Plants have different ways of **(reproducing, photosynthesis)**, or making new plants. In flowering plants, the seeds of new plants form inside **(flowers, leaves)**. In conifers, the seeds of the new plant form inside **(cones, leaves)**. A seed needs soil, space, and **(oxygen, water)** to grow into a new plant.

Chapter Review

Each of the following paragraphs tells about something you read in Chapter 2. Read each paragraph. Underline the word that makes each sentence correct.

Like plants, all animals are made of many **(cells, bones)**. Unlike plants, animals can't make their own food. They must eat other plants and animals. All animals have different parts called organs. Stomachs, brains, **(skin, hair)**, and bones are all organs.

There are many ways to group animals. One way is to group cold-blooded and warm-blooded animals. The body temperature of **(cold-blooded, warm-blooded)** animals changes with the outside temperature. Another way to group animals is by body parts. Animals that have a skeleton are called **(invertebrates, vertebrates)**.

All animals need oxygen, water, and food to live. To get energy from food, animals must **(like, digest)** it. The teeth, stomach, and intestines work together to break food down into tiny bits. The blood carries this food throughout the body.

Animals begin life as an egg. They have four stages in their life cycles. Adult animals are able to **(reproduce, think)**. Some animals lay eggs outside their bodies. Other animals keep eggs inside their **(pouches, bodies)**.

Humans are **(mammals, reptiles)**. Mammals are animals that have hair and feed their young with **(milk, meat)**. After birth, human babies are helpless. Babies grow into children. As children develop, they become taller and stronger.

Humans have two kinds of characteristics. Some are learned and some are inherited. Eye color is a characteristic that is **(learned, inherited)**. Playing the piano is a characteristic that is **(learned, inherited)**.

Name _____ Date _____

Chapter Review

Each of the following paragraphs tells about something you read in Chapter 3. Read each paragraph. Underline the word that makes each sentence correct.

You use your senses to learn about the world. You have the senses of sight, **(hearing, walking)**, smell, taste, and touch. Receptor cells are the cells that can sense different things such as colors, sounds, smells, and tastes.

The eyes, ears, nose, tongue, and skin are sense organs. They send signals about the outside world to your **(heart, brain)**. These signals move from the sense organs through thousands of **(nerve, organ)** cells.

The eyes have four main parts. These are the pupil, iris, lens, and retina. The pupil is the hole that lets light in. The iris is the **(white, colored)** part of the eye. Receptor cells in the eye send signals along the optic nerve to the brain. The ears have three main parts—the outer, middle, and inner ear. Sound waves pass through the **(eardrum, cochlea)** and then into the middle ear.

The receptor cells for taste are in the taste **(bulbs, buds)** on the tongue. The receptor cells that sense odors are called olfactory cells. These two senses work together. Skin is an important sense organ. Nerves just below the skin can sense cold, heat, pressure, deep pressure, and **(pain, light)**.

It is very important to protect your sense organs. You can do this by eating the right kinds of foods and getting the right amounts of exercise and rest. You can stay away from loud noises. Wear sunglasses and a hat and use sunscreen when out in the sun. Wear a **(coat, helmet)** when biking, skateboarding, or skating.

Name _____   Date _____

Chapter Review

Each of the following paragraphs tells about something you read in Chapter 4. Read each paragraph. Underline the word that makes each sentence correct.

All living things live in ecosystems. Forests, streams, oceans, and deserts are ecosystems. They are homes for many different animals and plants. Ecosystems also have **(nonliving, living)** things like water, rocks, and soil.

In ecosystems, energy is shared in a food chain. Plants are called producers because they make their own **(water, food)**. Animals are called consumers because they eat other living things. Animals that eat both plants and animals are called **(herbivores, omnivores)**. Tiny living things that eat dead animals and plants are called **(carnivores, decomposers)**.

Living things compete for things they need to live. Plants compete for sunlight, space, and **(food, water)**. Animals compete for food, water, and the best places to live.

Change is natural in ecosystems. Plants and animals grow and die. A fire or flood can quickly change or destroy a community. If every one of a kind of plant or animal is **(killed, hurt)** it becomes extinct. This change is **(permanent, temporary)**.

People harm ecosystems when they cut trees or create pollution. People help ecosystems by planting trees and by creating nature preserves. People also help protect ecosystems by **(reducing, increasing)** their use of things that cause pollution or by reusing or recycling products.

Name _____ Date _____

Chapter Review

Each of the following paragraphs tells about something you read in Chapter 5. Read each paragraph. Underline the word that makes each sentence correct.

Earth's surface has many landforms. Mountains are **(higher, flatter)** than hills. Low, flat areas that spread out for miles and miles are **(plains, plateaus)**.

Landforms are always changing. Rocks are broken and worn away by slow weathering. Wind and flowing water can also cause **(erosion, pollution)**. Earthquakes can cause landslides when the large plates in Earth's **(center, crust)** push against each other. Volcanoes erupt when melted rock from deep down inside Earth breaks through the crust.

Igneous rocks form when melted rock **(erodes, cools)**. Sedimentary rock forms when bits of rock, dead animals, and plants are pressed together. Metamorphic rock is formed when rock is pressed and **(heated, broken)** deep inside Earth.

The ocean floor also has landforms. Close to land is the continental **(shelf, valley)**. Farther out is the deeper open ocean. The dark, lifeless abyss is the **(widest, deepest)** part. Everywhere, ocean currents flow in different directions.

The ocean is important to us. We eat fish. We use **(oil, minerals)** from under the ocean floor. Ocean ships and tankers carry our supplies. People need to keep the ocean clean for all living things.

Chapter Review

Each of the following paragraphs tells about something you read in Chapter 6. Read each paragraph. Underline the word that makes each sentence correct.

Astronomers today use many tools to study objects in space. Optical telescopes collect **(sound, light)** waves. Radio telescopes collect radio waves, which astronomers study to learn about **(space, radios)**. Space probes travel into space and send back pictures and other information.

In our solar system, nine planets orbit the sun. They are pulled toward the sun by **(gravity, wind)**. In 365 days, Earth goes around the sun once. Earth also **(rotates, orbits)** on its axis one full turn every 24 hours.

The moon orbits Earth. It is much smaller than Earth and has no air or water. The moon reflects sunlight. Changes in the way it looks are called **(crescents, phases)**. Astronauts landed on the moon in 1969.

The inner planets are Mercury, Venus, Earth, and **(Mars, Jupiter)**. These planets have rocky crusts, iron cores, and atmospheres. Earth is the only planet we know that has **(life, mountains)**.

There are five outer planets. Jupiter, Saturn, Uranus, and Neptune are very **(small, large)**. Pluto is the smallest planet in the solar system. Comets and asteroids also orbit the sun. Comets are made of **(metal, ice)**. Asteroids are huge pieces of rock or metal. A shooting star is a meteor, which is a **(meteoroid, comet)** burning in Earth's atmosphere.

Name _____   Date _____

Chapter Review

Each of the following paragraphs tells about something
you read in Chapter 7. Read each paragraph. Underline
the word that makes each sentence correct.

We see colors because light has colors in it. The light that
is made of red, green, blue, and other colors is called
(**black, white**) light. You can see the colors in white light
by shining light through a (**window, prism**). Light gives
every object its color. When light hits an object, the
object's color is the light that is bounced back.

Light travels in a straight line until it hits an object.
When it hits an object, the object takes in, or absorbs,
some of the light. The object also (**reflects, reacts**), or
bounces back, some of the light. Light that passes through
an object is refracted. This is because when light passes
through an object it (**bends, strengthens**).

All sounds are caused by (**vibration, electricity**). Sounds
move in waves called sound waves. The highness or
lowness of a sound is called its (**volume, pitch**).

Magnets are special objects that pull or push other
magnets or pieces of metal. Magnets work because of an
unseen force called (**gravity, magnetism**). Magnets have
two ends, called (**poles, stubs**).

Electricity is an important kind of energy. It is used for
light, heat, communication, cooking, and many other
things. Electricity always travels in a circle. This circle is
called a (**round, circuit**) and can be in different sizes.
Some are very small like in a flashlight. Others are very
large, such as between a power plant and your home.

Focus on Science Level D

Unit Test

Darken the circle next to the correct answer.

1. The smallest part of a living thing is
   - Ⓐ a plant.
   - Ⓑ an egg.
   - Ⓒ a cell.
   - Ⓓ a stem.

2. Plants use light, carbon dioxide, and water to make food during
   - Ⓐ chlorophyll.
   - Ⓑ reproduction.
   - Ⓒ specialization.
   - Ⓓ photosynthesis.

3. What happens after a plant's eggs and pollen come together?
   - Ⓐ A plant flowers.
   - Ⓑ A seed forms.
   - Ⓒ A plant makes food.
   - Ⓓ A root forms.

4. What are animals that have backbones called?
   - Ⓐ warm-blooded
   - Ⓑ exoskeletons
   - Ⓒ vertebrates
   - Ⓓ invertebrates

5. To get energy from food, your body must
   - Ⓐ digest it.
   - Ⓑ mix it with carbon dioxide.
   - Ⓒ add oxygen to it.
   - Ⓓ add water to it.

6. Birth, growth, adulthood, and death are part of the
   - Ⓐ life cycle.
   - Ⓑ photosynthesis.
   - Ⓒ reproduction.
   - Ⓓ specialization.

7. Which animals have hair and feed their young with milk?
   - Ⓐ birds
   - Ⓒ invertebrates
   - Ⓑ mammals
   - Ⓓ fish

8. You can learn about the world around you through your
   - Ⓐ characteristics.
   - Ⓑ sense organs.
   - Ⓒ life cycle.
   - Ⓓ skeleton.

9. Cells that can sense color, sounds, and smell are
   - Ⓐ sense organs.
   - Ⓑ nerve cells.
   - Ⓒ odor cells.
   - Ⓓ receptor cells.

10. Four main parts of the eye are
    - Ⓐ pupil, iris, lens, retina.
    - Ⓑ cochlea, eardrum, middle ear, inner ear.
    - Ⓒ olfactory cells, odors, taste buds, tongue.
    - Ⓓ nervous system, brain, nerves, sense organs.

Unit Test

Darken the circle next to the correct answer.

1. A community of plants and animals in an area is
   - Ⓐ a territory.
   - Ⓑ an ecosystem.
   - Ⓒ a population.
   - Ⓓ a habitat.

2. What is harmful waste that can hurt an ecosystem?
   - Ⓐ decomposers
   - Ⓑ pollution
   - Ⓒ competition
   - Ⓓ extinct animals

3. People protect ecosystems by
   - Ⓐ recycling waste materials.
   - Ⓑ cutting down trees in ecosystems.
   - Ⓒ building roads through ecosystems.
   - Ⓓ drinking bottled water.

4. Earth's landforms are
   - Ⓐ rocks, sand, grass, and soil.
   - Ⓑ rocks, wind, snow, and ice.
   - Ⓒ wind, volcanoes, earthquakes, and landslides.
   - Ⓓ mountains, hills, plateaus, and plains.

5. The breaking and wearing away of landforms is called
   - Ⓐ the food chain.
   - Ⓑ cutting down.
   - Ⓒ reducing.
   - Ⓓ weathering.

6. Three different kinds of rock are
   - Ⓐ rough, smooth, uneven.
   - Ⓑ igneous, sedimentary, metamorphic.
   - Ⓒ pebbles, sand, seashells.
   - Ⓓ melted, squeezed, cooled.

7. Where is the longest mountain chain on Earth found?
   - Ⓐ in a forest ecosystem
   - Ⓑ on top of two large plateaus
   - Ⓒ on the bottom of the ocean
   - Ⓓ along the coast of China

8. To study objects in space, astronomers use
   - Ⓐ thermometers and weather balloons.
   - Ⓑ meteors and comets.
   - Ⓒ telescopes and space probes.
   - Ⓓ microscopes and magnifying glasses.

9. Our solar system is the sun and
   - Ⓐ Earth.
   - Ⓑ Earth with its moon.
   - Ⓒ all the planets.
   - Ⓓ everything that circles it.

10. What are huge pieces of rock or metal that orbit the sun called?
   - Ⓐ asteroids
   - Ⓑ comets
   - Ⓒ inner planets
   - Ⓓ moon phases

Unit Test

Darken the circle next to the correct answer.

1. We can see an object because light
   Ⓐ can pass through the object.
   Ⓑ is taken in by the object.
   Ⓒ is bent by the object.
   Ⓓ bounces off the object back to our eyes.

2. Which part of white light bounces off an object that looks red to us?
   Ⓐ the green part
   Ⓑ the blue part and the green part
   Ⓒ the red part
   Ⓓ all parts except the red part

3. Light that bounces back from an object is said to be
   Ⓐ absorbed.
   Ⓑ reflected.
   Ⓒ refracted.
   Ⓓ slowed down.

4. Why is light refracted when it passes from air into water?
   Ⓐ because it gets wet
   Ⓑ because it makes a rainbow
   Ⓒ because it cools off
   Ⓓ because it slows down

5. Sound travels as
   Ⓐ magnetism.
   Ⓑ vibrations.
   Ⓒ electricity.
   Ⓓ light energy.

6. The loudness or softness of sound is its
   Ⓐ volume.
   Ⓑ pitch.
   Ⓒ vibration.
   Ⓓ sound wave.

7. The two ends of a magnet are its
   Ⓐ circuit.
   Ⓑ magnetism.
   Ⓒ poles.
   Ⓓ push and pull.

8. When magnetic poles that are the same are put together, they always
   Ⓐ push away from each other.
   Ⓑ pull toward each other.
   Ⓒ are south poles.
   Ⓓ are one south pole and one north pole.

9. What kind of energy do people use to make light, heat their homes, and cook food?
   Ⓐ light
   Ⓑ magnetism
   Ⓒ sound
   Ⓓ electricity

10. Electricity travels in a circle called
    Ⓐ a battery.
    Ⓑ a circuit.
    Ⓒ a power plant.
    Ⓓ a bulb.

Focus on Science Level D

Answer Key

Answers to Problem Solving Blackline Masters

Chapter 1

The rings in the wood are wider in the middle and much closer together near the outside. The small size of the outer rings shows that there was less rainfall during the time just before the people left. It looks as if there was a long drought, which could have forced the people to leave.

Chapter 2

Answers will vary. Possible answers include:

Inherited Characteristics:
eye color, hair color, height, skin color, length and thickness of hands and fingers, size of feet, shape of nose and mouth

Learned Characteristics:
reading, speaking, singing, walking, playing a musical instrument, knowing how to play games and sports, understanding science, math, and other subjects

Chapter 3

Answers will vary. A response might be similar to this letter.

Dear Family:

My name is Jane Doe. I am a camp leader at Camp Lotsafun. This summer I will be Jimmy's group leader. I've been to camp for six years now and love it. I know that he will have a great time! To help make sure that he has fun, I want to tell you a few things that he should bring. We play outside a lot, so he should bring sunscreen and a hat. We also swim at the lake. He might like to bring goggles or earplugs. If he is going to be riding a bike or a skateboard, he must bring a helmet. It's a good idea to send his helmet even if you're not sure what he'll be doing. Of course, we have a trained nurse and all the group leaders know first aid, but you might pack something for poison ivy. Jimmy might also like to have sunglasses for the very bright days.

I look forward to meeting you and Jimmy in July.

Sincerely yours,

Chapter 4

1. Students should understand that clear-cutting creates erosion, destroys the forest, and is, in the long run, not economical.
2. Cut only a few trees at a time; plant new trees in the clear-cut area; find alternative sources for paper pulp.
3. Buy recycled pulp from a recycling center; make paper from cotton or other plants.

Chapter 5

1. inactive volcanoes covered with lots of plants and an active volcano with some lava hardening into rock
2. Volcanoes formed when molten rock erupted from deep inside Earth. The lava hardened to rock and soil formed on top. Plants grew in the soil. Rock is still forming as the volcano erupts.
3. One hundred years from now, all the volcanoes might be inactive and the whole area might be covered with plants. The mountains will still be visible. Or maybe one of the volcanoes will erupt again, destroying much of the plant life.

Chapter 6

The shadow on the sundial will move all day. It will be long in the morning, on the western side of the stick, shorten to nothing or almost nothing about noon, and lengthen towards the east in the afternoon. The earth rotates from west to east, and the sunlight hits Earth at different angles throughout the day.

Chapter 7

Make a compass by magnetizing a sewing needle from the sewing kit and floating it on a small piece of wood in a plastic cup of water. Be sure that there are no other metal objects nearby. When the magnetized needle comes to rest, it will be pointing north and south.

Answers to Chapter Review Blackline Masters

Chapter 1
food
leaves
cells
tissues
photosynthesis
oxygen
food
leaves
light
down
leaves
close
reproducing
flowers
cones
water

Chapter 2
cells
skin
cold-blooded
vertebrates
digest
reproduce
bodies
mammals
milk
inherited
learned

Chapter 3
hearing
brain
nerve
colored
eardrum
buds
pain
helmet

Chapter 4
nonliving
food
omnivores
decomposers
water
killed
permanent
reducing

Chapter 5
higher
plains
erosion
crust
cools
heated
shelf
deepest
oil

Chapter 6
light
space
gravity
rotates
phases
Mars
life
large
ice
meteoroid

Chapter 7
white
prism
reflects
bends
vibration
pitch
magnetism
poles
circuit

Unit Performance Project

A Storyboard About Life Cycles

Use the frame below to make a storyboard about
life cycles. Create a storyboard that shows the life cycle
of a plant or an animal. Be certain your storyboard has
both pictures and descriptions.

Name _____ Date _____

Unit Performance Project

Competition Within a Food Web

Create a one-meter square in a place you can revisit several times. Observe the plants and animals that use and compete for resources in the square. Visit the square 5 different times. Observe for at least 30 minutes each time. Keep a log of your observations. Date each observation.

After your last visit, use poster board to design and explain a food web that matches your observations.

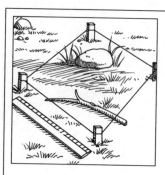

Unit Performance Project

A Sound Chart

You hear many sounds all around you. Some sounds are soft. Others are loud. Spend time inside and outside listening for sounds. Spend at least 15 minutes each time. Then use this chart to show how loud the different sounds were. Number 1 stands for very soft sounds. Number 10 stands for very loud sounds. Mark each sound on the correct place on the chart.

Sound Chart

10
9
8
7
6
5
4
3
2
1
0

FOCUS ON SCIENCE™

Unit Performance Project Rubrics

Unit 1: A Storyboard About Life Cycles

An **Outstanding** project

1—shows all stages in the life cycle, each represented by a picture or drawing.

2—shows all stages in correct order.

3—shows all stages correctly labeled or named and includes a brief description or explanation of each stage.

Outstanding = 3 out of the 3 points listed above

Good = 2 out of 3

Satisfactory = 1 out of 3

Unit 2: Competition Within a Food Web

An **Outstanding** project

1—shows a record of five 30-minute observations of plants and animals.

2—includes a visual representation of the results of the observations.

3—offers explanations for the relationships that exist in the food web.

Outstanding = 3 out of the 3 points listed above

Good = 2 out of 3

Satisfactory = 1 out of 3

Unit 3: A Sound Chart

An **Outstanding** project

1—includes a set of notes from two observational periods, one inside and one outside.

2—includes a chart that includes all of the objects the students recorded.

3—includes an accurate presentation of information in the chart.

Outstanding = 3 out of the 3 points listed above

Good = 2 out of 3

Satisfactory = 1 out of 3

FOCUS ON
SCIENCE™

Date

Dear Family:

Your child is now studying Chapter 1, *How Plants Live and Grow.* This book is divided into three units and seven chapters. The first chapter of Unit 1 introduces basic information about plants and the life cycle of plants. Your child will learn how plants get energy to grow, how plants change, and how plants reproduce.

You can help reinforce what your child is learning by reading the book with your child. Ask your child to tell you about the pictures and the diagrams in the chapter. You might ask him or her to read a few pages to you.

Below are some additional activities that you might want to complete with your child.

Thank you for your interest and support.

Sincerely,

A Seed Study

Plant a seed with your child. You can use the seed from an orange, a grapefruit, an apple, or a lemon. Place the seed in a bit of soil in a small pot. Place the pot on a windowsill. Help your child remember to make sure the seed has the water it needs to grow.

Observe Some Flowers

Visit a nursery, greenhouse, or another place where plants are sold. Help your child see that the flower is made of many small parts. See if your child can find the pollen in the flower. Help your child compare the blooming flower to one that has gone to seed.

_____

Fecha

Estimada familia:

Su hijo o hija ha comenzado a estudiar el Capítulo 1: *How Plants Live and Grow.* Este libro está dividido en tres unidades y siete capítulos. El primer capítulo de la Unidad 1 presenta información básica sobre las plantas y su ciclo de vida. Su hijo o hija aprenderá cómo las plantas obtienen su energía para crecer, cómo cambian y cómo se reproducen.

Pueden leer juntos el libro, para que su hijo o hija repase lo que está aprendiendo. Pídale que hable de los dibujos y diagramas que aparecen en el capítulo, y que lea en voz alta unas cuantas páginas.

A continuación presentamos actividades adicionales que pueden completar juntos.

Muchas gracias por su apoyo e interés.

Atentamente,

_____

Estudio de una semilla

Siembre una semilla con su hijo o hija. Pueden usar la semilla de una naranja, una toronja, una manzana o un limón. Coloquen la semilla con un poco de tierra en una maceta pequeña. Luego coloquen la maceta cerca de la ventana. Ayude a su hijo o hija a recordar que debe darle agua a la semilla para que crezca.

Observación de flores

Vayan de visita a un vivero, un invernadero u otro lugar donde vendan plantas. Muestre a su hijo o hija que una flor está formada de varias partes pequeñas. Pídale que trate de hallar el polen en la flor. También ayúdelo a distinguir una flor florecida de una que se ha transformado en semilla.

FOCUS ON
SCIENCE™

Date

Dear Family:

Your child is now studying Chapter 2, *How Animals Live and Grow.* This chapter has information about how animals grow and develop. Your child will learn how different kinds of animals are grouped; how animals get oxygen, water, and food; about animal life cycles; and how animals have both learned and inherited characteristics.

By reading the book together, you can help your child learn more about animals. Review illustrations, asking your child to tell you about them. You might ask your child to read a few pages aloud and talk about what he or she has read.

Below are two additional activities that you might want to complete with your child.

Thank you for your interest and support.

Sincerely,

A Baby Animal Study

Ask your child to find photographs of baby animals and their parents. You might like to paste the photos in a scrapbook. Use the photographs to talk about the differences and similarities between adult animals and their babies.

List Characteristics

Work with your child to list at least 20 of his or her characteristics. The list could include items such as hair and eye color, being able to read, or hand size. When the list is complete, help your child divide the characteristics into those that are learned and those that are inherited. As you do this, talk about why each trait fits best into its category.

_____

Fecha

Estimada familia:

Su hijo o hija ha comenzado a estudiar el Capítulo 2: *How Animals Live and Grow*. Este capítulo trata sobre el crecimiento y el desarrollo de los animales. Su hijo o hija aprenderá cómo están clasificados los animales, cómo obtienen el oxígeno, cómo hallan agua y alimento, cuáles son sus ciclos de vida. También aprenderá que los animales tienen características aprendidas y características heredadas.

Pueden leer juntos el libro, para que su hijo o hija aprenda más sobre los animales. Revisen juntos las ilustraciones y pídale que explique lo que significan. También puede pedirle que lea en voz alta unas cuantas páginas y que converse con usted sobre lo que ha leído.

A continuación presentamos actividades adicionales que pueden completar juntos.

Muchas gracias por su apoyo e interés.

Atentamente,

_____

Estudio de un animal bebé

Pida a su hijo o hija que busque fotografías de animales que estén junto a sus crías. Pegue las fotografías en un álbum. Use esas fotografías para conversar sobre las diferencias y similitudes entre los animales adultos y sus crías.

Lista de características

Prepare con su hijo o hija una lista de por lo menos 20 características de él o ella. La lista puede incluir aspectos tales como el color del cabello y de los ojos, el tamaño de la mano y si es capaz de leer. Cuando complete la lista, ayude a su hijo o hija a dividir las características en dos grupos: las que se aprenden y las que se heredan. Mientras hacen eso, conversen del por qué cada cualidad pertenece a una categoría determinada.

FOCUS ON
SCIENCE™

Date

Dear Family:

Your child is studying Chapter 3, *Your Senses.* This chapter tells about the senses of sight, hearing, smell, taste, and touch. The chapter also explains how the eyes, ears, nose, taste buds, and nerves work, and how we can protect the sense organs.

By reading the book together and discussing the information, you can reinforce what your child is learning. As you go through the chapter, use the diagrams of the nervous system, eyes, ears, taste buds, and receptor cells to help focus on important points.

Below are some additional activities that you might want to complete with your child.

Thank you for your interest and support.

Sincerely,

Taste the Difference

Provide different taste experiences for your child. Find foods for each of the four taste categories: sweet, salty, sour, and bitter. Give each food to your child, and ask him or her to identify the category to which it belongs. For example, you might give your child a raisin, a salty cracker, a bit of lemon, and a small piece of unsweetened baking chocolate.

A Journey of the Senses

Sit outside with your child. Ask your child to close his or her eyes and not to peek. Encourage your child to notice sounds, smells, and any touch sensations, such as the wind. Talk about how much we use our eyes and how much we depend upon the sense of sight.

Fecha

Estimada familia:

Su hijo o hija ha comenzado a estudiar el Capítulo 3: *Your Senses*. Este capítulo trata sobre los cinco sentidos: la vista, el oído, el olfato, el sabor y el tacto. El capítulo también explica cómo funcionan los ojos, los oídos, la nariz, las papilas gustativas y el sistema nervioso, y cómo podemos proteger esos órganos.

Pueden leer juntos el libro y conversar sobre lo que leen, para que su hijo o hija repase lo que está aprendiendo. Mientras revisan el capítulo, usen los diagramas del sistema nervioso, ojos, oídos, papilas gustativas y células receptoras para concentrarse en los puntos importantes.

A continuación presentamos actividades adicionales que pueden completar juntos.

Muchas gracias por su apoyo e interés.

Atentamente,

Saboree la diferencia

Dé la oportunidad a su hijo o hija de probar alimentos de distintos sabores. Busque alimentos que pertenezcan a cada una de las cuatro categorías de sabor: dulce, salado, agrio y amargo. Déle a probar cada alimento y pídale que identifique la categoría a la que pertenece. Por ejemplo, le puede dar una uva pasa, una galleta salada, un poco de limón y un trozo pequeño de chocolate sin azúcar.

Viaje de los sentidos

Siéntese con su hijo o hija afuera. Pídale que cierra sus ojos y que no mire a hurtadillas. Anímelo a percibir sonidos, olores y cualquier sensación táctil como el viento. Conversen sobre la importancia de los ojos y lo mucho que dependemos del sentido de la vista en nuestras vidas.

Focus on Science Level D

FOCUS ON
SCIENCE™

_____
Date

Dear Family:

Your child is now studying Chapter 4, *The Living Earth.* This chapter introduces information about ecosystems. Your child will learn that ecosystems are communities of many living things, how ecosystems support life, how they change naturally, and how they are changed by people.

You can help your child understand and remember these ideas by reading the chapter with your child. As you read, invite your child to tell you about the pictures and the diagrams. You might ask your child to read a few pages to you and to describe what he or she has learned in class.

Below are some additional activities that you might want to complete with your child.

Thank you for your interest and support.

Sincerely,

_____

A Waste Study

Invite your child to study the waste from this week's lunch. Ask him or her to bring home the paper and plastic wrappings from lunch. Collect the waste for a week and examine it. Ask your child for ideas about how to reduce the waste, recycle it, or reuse it.

Join a Community Cleanup

Spend an afternoon cleaning a nearby ecosystem with your child. Contact a local volunteer center or an ecology center to find out about scheduled beach, river, or trail cleanups. Help your child feel proud of his or her participation.

FOCUS ON
SCIENCE™

Fecha

Estimada Familia:

Su hijo o hija ha comenzado a estudiar el Capítulo 4: *The Living Earth*. Este capítulo trata sobre los sistemas ecológicos. En el capítulo aprenderá que los sistemas ecológicos son comunidades de muchos seres vivientes. También aprenderá cómo los sistemas ecológicos mantienen la vida, cómo cambian naturalmente y cómo los cambiamos los seres humanos.

Pueden leer juntos el capítulo, para que su hijo o hija comprenda y recuerde mejor los conceptos principales que ha aprendido. Mientras leen, pídale que converse sobre los dibujos y los diagramas. También puede pedirle que lea en voz alta unas cuantas páginas y que describa lo que ha aprendido en la clase.

A continuación presentamos actividades adicionales que pueden completar juntos.

Muchas gracias por su apoyo e interés.

Atentamente,

Estudio de desperdicios

Invite a su hijo o hija a estudiar durante esta semana los desperdicios de sus almuerzos. Pídale que lleve a casa las envolturas de papel y de plástico que venían con su almuerzo. Reúnan los desperdicios de los almuerzos de la semana y examínenlos. Luego pídale sugerencias de cómo reducir el desperdicio, cómo reciclarlo y cómo hacer para volverlo a usar.

Limpieza comunal

Dediquen una tarde a ayudar a limpiar un sistema ecológico en su comunidad. Comuníquese con un centro local de voluntarios o un centro de ecología para averiguar los horarios de limpieza de playas, ríos o senderos. Ayude a que su hijo o hija sienta orgullo de su participación.

FOCUS ON
SCIENCE™

_____
Date

Dear Family:

Your child has begun studying Chapter 5, *Earth's Surface.* This chapter introduces basic information about landforms and geology. Your child will learn the names and shapes of Earth's landforms, as well as how these landforms are formed and are changed.

The diagrams and the pictures in the book will help your child understand new concepts in geology. You can support your child's exploration by looking at these pictures with him or her. You might also ask your child to read to you from the text.

Below are some additional activities that you might want to complete with your child.

Thank you for your interest and support.

Sincerely,

_____

A Bird's Eye View

Take your child to a place where there is a good view of the surrounding area. You can climb a hill or look out the window of a tall building. Point out landforms and bodies of water. Help your child become familiar with landforms in your area.

Watch a Video

View a video of an earthquake or a volcanic eruption with your child. You might rent a *National Geographic* Video from a video store, or you may find one in your local library. Talk about the events in the film. Ask your child to describe them in his or her own words.

Fecha

Estimada familia:

Su hijo o hija ha comenzado a estudiar el Capítulo 5: *Earth's Surface*. Este capítulo presenta información básica sobre los accidentes geográficos y la geología. En el capítulo aprenderá los nombres y las diversas formas de los accidentes geográficos del planeta, y también aprenderá cómo se forman y cambian esos accidentes geográficos con el tiempo.

Pueden ver los dibujos y diagramas del libro juntos para ayudar a su hijo o hija a comprender nuevos conceptos de geología. También puede pedirle que lea en voz alta unas cuantas páginas.

A continuación presentamos actividades adicionales que pueden completar juntos.

Muchas gracias por su apoyo e interés.

Atentamente,

Desde lo alto

Lleve a su hijo o hija a un lugar donde haya una buena vista de los alrededores. Suban a una colina o miren por la ventana de un edificio alto. Señale los accidentes geográficos y las extensiones de agua que puedan ver. Ayude a su hijo o hija a familiarizarse con los accidentes geográficos de la región donde viven.

Mire un video

Vean juntos un video de un terremoto o de una erupción volcánica. Puede alquilar un video de la *National Geographic* en una tienda de videos, o puede que su biblioteca local tenga una copia. Conversen sobre lo que sucede en la película y pídale que lo describa en sus propias palabras.

FOCUS ON
SCIENCE™

_____

Date

Dear Family:

    Your child is now studying Chapter 6, *Our Solar System.* This chapter tells about our solar system. Your child will learn about the nine planets that orbit our sun, and other solid objects that move within our solar system.

    To reinforce the concepts in this chapter, please read the book with your child. You might ask your child to read several pages to you. Ask your child questions about the text and have him or her tell you about the illustrations.

    Below are some additional activities that you might want to complete with your child.

    Thank you for your interest and support.

Sincerely,

_____

A Sky Study

Study the night sky with your child. In the newspaper, check when the moon rises. Look at the moon several nights in a row and talk about the phases. If possible, look at the moon's craters through binoculars. You might also use an astronomy guide to locate several planets.

Visit a Planetarium

Take your child to a planetarium show. Natural history museums and many colleges have planetariums. Find out when there is a show about our solar system. Encourage your child to take a list of questions to ask about our solar system to the planetarium.

_____
Fecha

Estimada familia:

Su hijo o hija ha comenzado a estudiar el Capítulo 6: *Our Solar System*. Este capítulo trata sobre nuestro sistema solar. Su hijo o hija, aprenderá acerca de los nueve planetas que giran alrededor del sol y de otros cuerpos celestes que se mueven dentro del sistema solar.

Pueden leer juntos el libro, para que su hijo o hija repase los conceptos. También puede pedirle que lea en voz alta unas cuantas páginas. Hágale preguntas sobre lo leído y pídale que explique las ilustraciones del capítulo.

A continuación presentamos actividades adicionales que pueden completar juntos.

Muchas gracias por su apoyo e interés.

Atentamente,

_____

Estudio del cielo

Observe el cielo nocturno con su hijo o hija. Averigüe en el periódico a qué hora sale la luna. Durante varias noches consecutivas, observen la luna y hablen de las fases lunares que observen. Si es posible, usen binoculares para observar los cráteres de la luna. También podrían usar una guía astronómica para ubicar a varios planetas.

Visita a un planetario

Lleve a su hijo o hija a una presentación en el planetario. Los museos de historia natural y muchas universidades tienen planetarios. Averigüe cuándo habrá una presentación sobre nuestro sistema solar. Anime a su hijo o hija a llevar al planetario una lista de preguntas sobre nuestro sistema solar.

FOCUS ON
SCIENCE™

Date

Dear Family:

Your child is now studying Chapter 7, *Energy,* the final chapter in the book. This chapter covers different forms of energy. Your child will learn about light, sound, magnets, and electricity. Some of the topics in this chapter include how light travels and how it is affected by a prism, how sound travels, and how all magnets have two poles.

You can help reinforce what your child is learning by reading the chapter together. As you read about the different forms of energy, ask your child to talk about how light and sound travel and some of the ways that electricity is used. You might ask him or her to read a few pages to you.

Below are some additional activities that you might want to complete with your child.

Thank you for your interest and support.

Sincerely,

A Prism Painting

Use a prism or a crystal that breaks light into colors. Have your child place it in direct sunlight and notice the colors that are produced. Then, ask your child to make a drawing or painting of the prism colors, copying their exact order.

The Speed of Light, the Speed of Sound

Have two groups of people stand in sight of each other but at least 100 yards apart. Then have each group take turns yelling a short sound in unison as they raise their arms. Have the other group note the event they experience first: the sound of the yell or the sight of the arms being raised. If the groups stand farther apart, the difference between light and sound will be greater.

FOCUS ON
SCIENCE™

Fecha

Estimada familia:

Su hijo o hija ha comenzado a estudiar el Capítulo 7: *Energy*. Este es el último capítulo del libro y trata sobre las distintas formas de energía que existen. En el capítulo, aprenderá sobre la luz, el sonido, los imanes y la electricidad. Los temas en este capítulo incluyen: cómo viaja la luz, el efecto de la luz en un prisma, cómo viaja el sonido y por qué todos los imanes tienen dos polos.

Pueden leer el libro juntos, para que su hijo o hija repase lo que está aprendiendo. Mientras leen sobre las distintas formas de energía que existen, puede pedirle que le explique cómo viaja la luz y el sonido, y cómo usamos la electricidad hoy en día. Luego, pídale que lea en voz alta unas cuantas páginas.

A continuación presentamos actividades adicionales que pueden completar juntos.

Muchas gracias por su apoyo e interés.

Atentamente,

La pintura de un prisma

Use un prisma o un cristal que divida la luz en colores. Pida a su hijo o hija que lo coloque directamente al sol y que observe los colores que se producen. Luego pídale que pinte los colores del prisma en el mismo orden en que aparecen al verlos al sol.

La velocidad de la luz y la velocidad del sonido

Organice a dos grupos de personas, para que se paren uno frente a otro, a unas 100 yardas de distancia (unos 90 metros). Luego pida a los grupos que se turnen para gritar al tiempo un sonido corto, y que a la vez levanten los brazos. Pida a los miembros de otro grupo que observen el evento y que digan que ocurrió primero para ellos: el grito o los brazos que se levantaron. Si los grupos se separan aún más, la diferencia entre la luz y el sonido será mayor.